OVER TO Y

REPORTS FROM CO!

GH00482826

Contents

Our Calling

INTRODUCTION

Conference 1999 received a report from the Methodist Council (Agenda pages 617-620) which summarised work done on this issue in the connexional year 1998/99. It agreed to the appointment of a Strategic Goals Planning Group to take the process forward. The Conference report noted that in the autumn of 1998 many individuals and churches, and some circuits, responded to an immediate invitation to participate in a process of identifying the Church's Strategic Goals. Every one of those responses has been carefully read.

1. **The outcomes we dream about in the group which has prepared the material**

   The whole Church rediscovers a shared vision of what the Church is for.

   In each local situation priorities come into focus, with imagination and energy released to achieve identified plans and targets.

   Significant changes of culture take place – flexible and creative applications of the gospel to the Church's work in contemporary society; liberation from tired traditions and the Methodist obsession with procedures and rules ('CPD and all that').

   A greater diversity of response to local situations is complemented by a strong sense of pulling together throughout the connexion in pursuit of our shared vision.

2. **Use of language**

   This work started with talk of Strategic Goals. That was shorthand and not popular. We gladly leave it behind, in favour of more suggestive vocabulary: a vision of what the Church is for and where we are going.

3. **What's new?**

   We have attempted only to crystallise what we all know about the Church in our heart of hearts. It would be nice to think we have expressed ourselves without too much jargon. We hope everyone can recognise the obvious links with people who have walked this path before us.

   We put weight on the process we hope our material could trigger in every church. Local ownership of this process and its outcomes is everything. Courage to see what is important, to go for it and to leave behind what is secondary will make the difference. And it does not matter if another church nearby, inevitably in a different context, comes up with something different.

   What we seek to facilitate is for every level of the Church – for the Conference, the Methodist Council, the connexional Team, districts and circuits as well as for the local churches. We are bound together by a single calling and a shared vision.

4. How shall we get things moving?

4.1 We want to make second nature among Methodists (and partners from other denominations who share our life at local level) the words which crystallise our vision of what the church is for.

The Church exists to

- **Increase awareness of God's presence and to celebrate God's Love**

- **Help people to grow and learn as Christians, through mutual support and care**

- **Be a good neighbour to people in need and to challenge injustice**

- **Make more followers of Jesus Christ**

To assist the memory, these words can be further condensed to read:

The Church is for

WORSHIP, LEARNING & CARING, SERVICE, EVANGELISM

4.2 We can help one another to absorb this shared vision in many ways. For example:

- Posters in churches and church halls.

- Everyone on our Community Roll and everyone who is interested in the Methodist Church can have a bookmark or a small card with the words of our shared vision printed on it.

- We can practise shaping the prayers of the Church within this framework week by week.

4.3 There will be a leaflet for every Methodist and for ecumenical friends. A provisional draft is included below. It has been drawn up to suggest a process, not to prescribe one. The questions under each main heading are indicative only. We do not pretend they are comprehensive, or perfectly worded. Our belief is that they are good enough to get the process underway. They can be adapted, edited or replaced by a church's own questions. The one exception, we suggest, is the final question in each section: "What are our plans and targets for…over the next year?"

We believe a simple resource of this kind can trigger a serious review of priorities in each situation, an exploration of initiatives which might be taken locally and a better use of resources. Good ideas can be turned into specific plans and targets. Twelve months later each local church can see where it has got to, look again at its aims, its resources and its environment, and revise its plans. What happens is always in the hands of the local church. And so the process rolls on year by year.

The strength of the process lies in the confidence we may feel that throughout the connexion we share a vision of what the church is for, and we all judge ourselves as we see fit against that vision.

4.4 To assist the process we are preparing a Leader's Pack. This will contain guidelines on how to use the leaflet locally and at circuit, district and connexional levels. It may also contain supplementary materials for those who wish to read them: about possible outcomes of the process if it becomes an annual part of the Church's life; about the core principles we need to hold on to as the process develops; and about the changes in society which require fresh understandings of Christian witness and mission.

4.5 We intend to inaugurate a training programme operating on a 'cascade down' system.

4.6 We shall need a monitoring process to review outcomes and to develop processes over, say, a five year period.

4.7 Some churches will want to develop a much more wide-ranging, thorough and systematic understanding of their environment and their own skills and resources. The connexional Team has already prepared a significant resource, provisionally entitled "Pilgrims Way", to meet such a need. It will be available from the Resourcing Mission Office in Manchester, who will also advise about people who can work with churches to put it into practice. Some ecumenical resources covering similar ground are also available, e.g. "Bridges of Hope" (CTE).

4.8 We anticipate that our own resources, all produced to show a family likeness to one another, will be available in January 2001.

5. **Prepared by:** Roger Dawe, Ermal Kirby, Peter White, Kate Woodhouse and David Deeks (convenor).

DRAFT LEAFLET:

THE METHODIST CHURCH

OUR CALLING

... TO FULFIL

What is the Church for and where are we going?

The calling of the Methodist Church is to respond to the
gospel of God's love in Christ and to live out its
discipleship in worship and mission

To fulfil our calling we need to develop plans of action at every level of the Church. We do this within a framework set by a shared vision.

The Church exists to:

- **increase awareness of God's presence and to celebrate God's love**

- **help people to grow and learn as Christians, through mutual support and care**

- **be a good neighbour to people in need and to challenge injustice**

- **make more followers of Jesus Christ**

OUR VISION

The Church exists to increase awareness of God's presence and to celebrate God's love

- What helps us to centre our worship on God?

- Where and when do we feel the presence of God? How can these experiences enrich services of worship?

- What motivates us to study the Bible?

- What helps us to express awe and wonder, thankfulness and praise, and love towards God? How can we use resources from the worldwide Church?

- What would help our worship to make sense to people who come only occasionally?

- Can we improve the comfort and décor of our surroundings and the welcome for people with disabilities?

- Is our worship much the same all the time? Should we explore styles and traditions of worship from other denominations and other parts of the world?

What are our plans and targets for improving our worship over the next year?

The Church exists to help people to grow and learn as Christians, through mutual support and care

- What church activities help us most to deepen our faith in God?

- How effective are our small groups, in linking faith to everyday life?

- How do we learn about the challenges of Christian life today from churches elsewhere in Britain and the wider world?

- Are there peripheral activities we should stop, to make time for our training and learning needs?

- What activities make it easy for others to join us? What links do we have with groups using our premises?

- What do we expect from our pastors? What do we expect from one another by way of support and care? Do we notice or care about those who drift away or leave?

What are our plans and targets for developing our life together over the next year?

OUR VISION

The Church exists to be a good neighbour to people in need and to challenge injustice

- How do we discover the needs in our community and respond to them?

- Who is involved in service to the community through charities or community groups? Are there opportunities for more of us to become involved? How do we give attention to the moral issues raised by daily work?

- Do we share with one another our concerns about things which do not seem right, or cause trouble in our community, or appear unjust?

- How do we challenge injustice in other parts of the world?

- Are we making the best use of our premises and our money for service to the community? Are we wasting resources? Are we spending our time and resources in ways which are consistent with our beliefs and values?

- How does the life of our community, and our involvement in it, feature in the prayers of the church?

What are our plans and targets for improving our community involvement over the next year?

The Church exists to make more followers of Jesus Christ

- How do we develop friendly attitudes towards everyone we meet?

- Do we have a clear message? Are the words we use straightforward and meaningful to those outside the Church?

- What attracts others to the Christian faith? Are there initiatives we could take to present our convictions? Can we do this with Christians of other denominations? Where should the focus be – on church premises, or in the community?

- How can we learn about effective witness from Christians in other cultures?

- What can we do to make our premises more welcoming?

- Should we consider planting a new congregation in this locality?

What are our plans and targets for making more followers of Jesus Christ over the next year?

RESOLUTIONS

34/1. The Conference endorses the vision of what the church is for, particularly as set out in 4.1.

34/2. The Conference calls on churches, circuits, districts and connexional bodies to develop the process entitled "Our Calling to Fulfil" over the next few years.

34/3. The Conference directs the Methodist Council annually to monitor outcomes and to authorise changes to facilitate the process at every level of the Church.

The Methodist Church's Environmental Policy

INTRODUCTION

This policy seeks to identify principles to assist the Methodist Church in translating into action its affirmation that mission includes 'caring for the earth' in the life of the Church at national and local level.

It has been prepared in the context of a Notice of Motion proposed at the 1998 Scarborough Conference and referred to the connexional Team without debate:

> The Conference directs the Methodist Council to prepare a Draft Environmental Policy for the Methodist Church. Such a policy statement should relate to all relevant areas of the Church's life.

> This statement should:

> i. spell out a commitment to act responsibly on matters of environmental concern

> ii. identify ways in which this commitment can be translated into action

> iii. identify the means by which progress can be measured

> The Methodist Council to report to the Conference in 2000.

The proposer and a small group of people drawn initially from the Darlington and Newcastle Districts have co-operated with the Secretary for International Affairs.

CARING FOR THE EARTH

1.   The Methodist Church affirms that Christian mission includes caring for God's earth and will endeavour to develop both the theology and practical implications of this on a continuing basis.

2.   The Biblical creation stories give human beings privilege and responsibility in relation to the earth and every living creature. We are called to be partners with the rest of creation and co-partners in the ongoing creative and renewing activity of God. Such partnership goes wrong when human beings act as if the whole earth were simply for their present benefit. God's way, revealed in the Bible and particularly in the life, death and resurrection of Christ, is a generous sharing of the divine love to serve the needs of God's creation until it reaches its fulfilment.

3.   Christian mission includes sharing in putting right the relationships within God's creation that have gone wrong, and growing towards the balance and good stewardship envisaged in the Biblical vision of the world as it is meant to be.

4.   The Methodist people are challenged and encouraged to care for the earth by following sustainable practice and taking into account global and local environmental considerations for present and future generations

- in the conservation and use of resources in the Church and at home
- in helping to develop more sustainable lifestyles
- in active involvement in Local Agenda 21* and other community initiatives
- in concerns for action on global environmental issues

5.   To help the Methodist people to fulfil this commitment, this policy identifies objectives relating to six aspects of the environment. The objectives are considered relevant to individual lifestyles, the ongoing life of the Church and to the construction, maintenance and use of church buildings.

Action in working towards achievement of the objectives should have regard to:

- the challenge of meeting the needs of the present without compromising the ability of future generations to meet their needs
- the potential for harnessing the skills, expertise and enthusiasm of the Methodist people
- the opportunities for co-operation and joint initiatives with other Churches or environmental initiatives and of the potential to contribute Methodist insights, including those arising from the connexional structure and shared ministry
- the effectiveness of the overall mission of the Church and the overall demands upon Methodist budgets
- the valuable contribution of small steps by individuals as well as major initiatives

6.   The connexional Team will keep this policy under review. Progress towards achievement of the principles and objectives will also be kept under review by the Methodist Council in relation to the work of the connexional Team. Districts and Circuits will be encouraged to support and encourage the pursuit of the objectives at the local church level. For significant change to take place, monitoring of plans and targets will be essential at every level of the Church's life.

7.   This policy contains a commitment to co-operation and joint initiatives with other Churches. To this end close contact is being maintained, in particular, with the Eco-Congregation Project. This project, based in Wigan, is jointly sponsored by Going for Green and the Churches Together in Britain and Ireland's Environmental Issues Network and is led by The Revd Dr David Pickering.   A pilot project, in which three Methodist churches in the Darlington District are involved, will be completed in early 2000 prior to the official launch of the Eco-Congregation project in September 2000. Part of the pilot phase will be the testing of the usefulness of material already available

i. The United Reformed Church's *Roots and Branches* pack.

ii. Christian Ecology Link's *Sustainability* pack, as well as the Christian Ecology Link Millennium Certificate Award Scheme.

iii. London and Southwark Diocese of the Church of England: *Caring for God's World (Practical Steps to becoming an Environmentally Friendly Church for the new Millennium)*

* Agenda 21 /Local Agenda 21 – an agenda which developed out of the 1992 United Nations Earth Summit (held in Rio, Brazil). Agenda 21 means 'an agenda for the 21st century'. Its aim is to promote development, which respects the environment and the needs of future generations. Much of the responsibility for the development and implementation of Agenda 21 is at national level but each Local Authority is also required to develop a set of Local Agenda 21 policies promoting sustainable development. Local Authorities are required to consult people and groups and this is where the churches can play a role.

Environmental Policy Objectives

Awareness and Commitment

- to promote awareness within Methodist people of these principles and objectives and of the values underlying them
- to ensure that Methodist Church employees and office holders are familiar with and implement this environmental commitment and its objectives
- to ensure that Methodist Church activities comply with all relevant environmental regulations

Energy and Water

- to ensure energy is used efficiently and wherever possible reduce its use
- to encourage the increased use of renewable energy
- to use water efficiently and with care
- to avoid pollutants entering the drainage system

Waste

- to reduce the production of material waste including unnecessary packaging
- to encourage re-use, repair and recycling of materials including organic waste
- to dispose of waste in a safe and responsible way

Materials and Resources

- to buy products which are made in accordance with the principle of using material in a sustainable way and to use locally-made goods where practicable
- to take into account the lifetime costs of materials when repairing, altering or rebuilding premises
- to maximise the proportion of paper used from sustainable sources and recycled materials

- to offer electronic communication as an alternative to paper for those who are suitably equipped
- to show concern for the environmental quality of food production systems and the equitable global distribution of food

Natural and Built Environment

- to take appropriate opportunities to conserve and enhance the natural and built environment including Methodist Heritage Sites
- to be aware of local planning developments
- to be sensitive to the impact of church activities on the local environment

Travel

- to make every effort to reduce air pollution and energy consumption resulting from the use of the car by avoidance of unnecessary travel and the use of energy efficient vehicles
- to explore undertaking the work of the Church in ways which reduce the need for travel particularly by car and allow for the possibility of and encourage access by public transport, cycle and on foot
- to share car transport where possible
- to support the expansion of good quality public transport, the provision of improved facilities for cyclists and pedestrians and local Green Travel Programmes.

RESOLUTIONS

2/1. The Conference adopts the policy 'Caring for the Earth', endorses its policy objectives and urges individual Methodists and Methodist churches to become aware of these objectives and to integrate them both into individual lifestyles and into the ongoing life of the church especially in relation to the construction, maintenance and use of church buildings.

2/2. The Conference gives authority for the Environmental Policy, as it may from time to time be reviewed and amended, to be used by churches for submission in applications for grants from the Landfill Tax Credit Scheme.

EPISKOPÉ AND EPISCOPACY

CONTENTS

A. INTRODUCTION

1. The Conference of 1997 adopted Notice of Motion 14:

   In order to enhance and develop discussions between the Methodist Church and the Church of England, the Church in Wales and the Scottish Episcopal Church, the Conference directs the Faith and Order Committee to clarify British Methodism's understanding of episcopacy and report to the Conference of 1998.

2. The Faith and Order Committee presented to the 1998 Conference a report which quoted extensively from the many statements about episcopacy which had been made in Methodist documents since the time of Methodist union. The Conference adopted the Committee's report and the following resolution:

   The Conference directs the Faith and Order Committee to bring to the Conference of 2000 a further report on episcopacy which:

   (i)   explores the understanding of corporate and personal oversight implied by our present connexional and district practice;

   (ii) explores models of the episcopate from the world-wide church;

   and on the basis of (i) and (ii)

   (iii) proposes to the Conference guidelines on issues of oversight, including those concerning bishops, which may guide Methodist representatives in ecumenical conversations and assist the development of our own structures.

3. The present report seeks to address the issues raised in the direction given to the Committee by the 1998 Conference.

B. TERMINOLOGY

4. It is important to distinguish from the outset between '*episkopé*' (the Greek word for 'oversight') and 'episcopacy', which refers to the oversight exercised by bishops. Generally, it is only those Churches which include the office of bishop within their structures which are called 'episcopal'.

5. *Episkopé* is exercised in all Christian communions, whether or not they are 'episcopal' churches. Thus episcopacy is not essential to ensure *episkopé*, though it is highly valued by the majority of Christian Churches.

6. The words 'oversight' and '*episkopé*' themselves convey a range of meanings. Some of these are given focus in the biblical image of the shepherd, which speaks of pastoral care and a concern for unity; it also speaks of leadership, enabling the Church to share in God's mission and maintaining and developing structures appropriate to that task. The exercise of *episkopé* also reminds the Church of its roots in Scripture and

tradition and encourages it to be open to the Spirit's leading in the contemporary context. *Episkopé* includes the exercise of authority, a sometimes uncongenial concept which is nevertheless required by church order.

7. Some episcopal Churches (notably the Orthodox, Roman Catholic and Anglican Churches) claim that their bishops belong to the 'historic episcopate' or stand in the 'historic succession':

> Within Anglicanism, the historic episcopate denotes the continuity of oversight in the Church through the ages from the earliest days, expressed in a personal episcopal ministry, the intention of which is to safeguard, transmit, and restate in every generation the apostolic faith delivered once for all to the saints.[1]

Other Churches which have bishops, such as the United Methodist Church, do not claim to be in 'the historic succession'. In Part E of this report, where various models of episcopacy are to be considered, it will be important to distinguish between those churches which make the claim and those that do not.

8. The very important World Council of Churches Faith and Order paper, *Baptism, Eucharist and Ministry* (*BEM*), speaks of ordained ministry being exercised in 'a personal, collegial and communal way'.[2] Since the publication of *BEM*, these three terms have increasingly been used in the discussion of ministries of oversight (*episkopé*). 'Personal' is self-explanatory. 'Collegial' oversight entails a group of people (usually ordained, and, indeed, ordained to the same order of ministry) jointly exercising *episkopé*. An English example is the House of Bishops of the Church of England. 'Communal' *episkopé* is exercised by a council or assembly, which may to a greater or lesser extent be 'democratically' elected, and which may include both lay and ordained people. The Methodist Conference is an example. The word 'corporate' is sometimes used in place of 'communal' in this context, as it is in the resolution (see 2 above) adopted by the 1998 Conference. In this report, the terms 'corporate' and 'communal' are used interchangeably.

9. The words 'Connexion' and 'connexional' are so familiar to Methodists that it may seem strange to refer to them in this section about terminology. Yet it is important to note that both words, and especially the adjective, can be used in two ways. The Connexion is usually taken to mean the whole of the British Methodist Church, embracing every District, Circuit and local church. There is another usage, however, in which the Connexion is distinguished from the Districts, Circuits and local churches, as in references to the Church 'at connexional level', as opposed, say, to 'District level'. Both usages are present in this report; it is hoped that in every case the context will make the meaning clear.

C. THE EXERCISE OF *EPISKOPÉ* IN BRITISH METHODISM

1. Communal *Episkopé*

a) The Conference

10. Any treatment of the Methodist experience of *episkopé* must begin with the Conference. The early Methodist Conferences were dominated by John Wesley, who set the agenda, summed up the conversation (the conferring) that ensued, and at the end announced what the programme or policy was to be. One preacher, after the 1774 Conference, was heard to remark: 'Mr Wesley seemed to do all the business himself.'[3] But Wesley believed that his power was God-given. As far as he was concerned, the Conference had no rights other than those which he conferred upon it. As he said:

> I myself sent for these, of my own free choice; and I sent for them to advise, not *govern* me. Neither did I at any one of those times divest myself of any part of that power above described, which the Providence of God had cast upon me, without any design or choice of mine.[4]

Clearly, then, the first form of *episkopé* to appear in Methodism was personal *episkopé*, the ministry of oversight (both pastoral and authoritative) of one man. But by Wesley's express design, that was to change after his death.

11. After Wesley's death, the Conference was given legal continuity by the Deed of Declaration, which Wesley had executed in 1784 to bestow upon the Legal Hundred those powers which he himself had held. The Legal Hundred (whose original members were selected by Wesley to provide a cross-section of the itinerant preachers) was the 'official' Conference, though other preachers were eligible to attend and it was the whole Conference which exercised general oversight within the Connexion. From that time onwards, the Conference exercised, as it still exercises, *episkopé* over the people called Methodists.

12. Though the character and constitution of the Conference has changed over time, the Conference continues to exercise a corporate rôle of *episkopé* over the connexion. This can be illustrated in a number of ways. First, the Conference exercises *episkopé* by directing and leading the Church's thoughts and actions. It makes authoritative statements on matters of faith and order, thus seeking to preserve and transmit the apostolic faith, and on social and ethical issues. It also seeks to discern the will of God in the world and to enable the Methodist people to respond to their missionary calling.

13. Second, subject to, and indeed in accordance with, the Methodist Church Act and other legal instruments, it is the Conference which can and does establish the constitution of Methodism at every level. In the case of significant changes in polity, the 33 Districts (and sometimes the Circuits and local churches) are consulted. But the final word rests with the Conference.

14. Third, we may consider the Conference's rôle in relation to ordained ministry. It is the Conference which approves those who are to be trained for diaconal or presbyteral ministry. It is the Conference which admits them, in due course, into full connexion with itself and which authorizes their ordination. Those who ordain do so only with the specific authority of the Conference to ordain named individuals. Almost all ordinations take place during the annual meeting of the Conference, in the region where the Conference is meeting, rather than in the Districts in which the ordinands serve. It is the Conference which stations the ministers and deacons. In all these matters, the Conference acts on the advice of other bodies – the Connexional Candidates Selection Committee, or the Stationing Committee, for example. But in every case it is the act of the Conference itself which is decisive.

15. Fourth, all who preside at Holy Communion in Methodism are authorized by the Conference to do so – ministers, by virtue of their ordination which took place on the authority of the Conference, ministers of other communions who are 'recognized and regarded' or 'authorized' by the Conference, and, exceptionally, lay persons or deacons who, where eucharistic deprivation would otherwise exist, are authorized by name by the Conference, with the matter subject to annual review.

16. Between the Conferences, the Methodist Council performs an oversight rôle. The Council is authorized to act on behalf of the Conference and is charged

> to keep in constant review the life of the Methodist Church, to study its work and witness throughout the Connexion, to indicate what changes are necessary or what steps should be taken to make the work of the Church more effective, to give spiritual leadership to the Church. [5]

In discharging its responsibilities, the Council is to ensure that the decisions of the Conference are fully implemented and to supervise the general work of the connexional Team. [6] Thus it may be said that the Council exercises delegated *episkopé* on behalf of the Conference.

b) The Circuit and the Local Church

17. Moving away from the Conference, it is important to note that at every other level of Methodism's life, some sort of communal *episkopé* is exercised too. Each local church has its Church Council, which

> has authority and oversight over the whole area of the ministry of the church, including the management of its property. Aims and methods, the determination and pursuit of policy and the deployment of available resources are its proper responsibility. [7]

18. Yet in terms of oversight, the rôle of the Circuit is even more significant. To quote from *Called to Love and Praise*, a Statement adopted by the 1999 Conference:

> The grouping of local churches in Circuits reflects the Methodist belief that no local church is an autonomous unit complete in itself. Rather, it is linked essentially and structurally to the wider Church. Circuit structures represent interdependence, relatedness, mutual responsibility and submission to mutual jurisdiction. Indeed, the Circuit, rather than the local church, has been the primary church unit in British Methodism. The appointment of Superintendent Ministers, with overall responsibility for the sharing within the Circuit of pastoral work, and for the preaching plan indicates the communal, interdependent character of the Church. The Circuit system also makes possible the deployment of resources in an area wider than that of the local church.[8]

19. This report will consider the rôle of the Superintendent Minister later. But first, it is instructive to look at the *episkopé* which belongs to the Circuit Meeting. This body is made up of the ministers and deacons appointed to the Circuit, various circuit officers, and representatives of each local church. It is the Circuit Meeting, not the local church, which invites ministers to serve in a Circuit (though such invitations are dependent upon the approval of the Conference, which, in the last analysis, stations ministers). It is the Circuits which provide funds for the stipends of ministers, from contributions received from the local churches. The Circuit is

> the primary unit in which local churches express and experience their interconnexion in the Body of Christ, for purposes of mission, mutual encouragement and help.[9]

> The Circuit Meeting . . . shall exercise that combination of spiritual leadership and administrative efficiency which will enable the Circuit to fulfil its purposes . . . and shall act as the focal point of the working fellowship of the churches in the Circuit, overseeing their pastoral, training and evangelistic work.[10]

c) The District

20. There are approximately 660 Circuits, with an average of ten local churches in each. Each Circuit in turn belongs to a District, of which there are 33 (not counting overseas Districts). This much larger unit is 'an expression, over a wider geographical area than the Circuit, of the connexional character of the Church'.[11] It

> . . . serves the local churches and Circuits and the Conference in the support, deployment and oversight of the various ministries of the Church, and in programmes of training.[12]

21. The District relates both to the Conference and to the Circuits. The District Synod, in its Representative Session, is the forum in which aspects of the agenda of the Conference are received in a more localized setting and issues affecting the life of the Circuits are discussed. The Synod orders District affairs and develops District policy. Unlike the

Conference, the Synod cannot direct the Circuits, except in some matters of finance and property, but by exploring important issues and by fellowship and sharing it has the capacity to lead and inspire. Most of its lay members are representatives from the Circuits, but all ministers and deacons in the active work and probationers are required to attend, unless given a dispensation from doing so. It is to the Synods that the Conference refers proposals for significant changes of polity. It is by the Synods that the vast majority of members of the Conference are appointed.

22. It is clear that, at four levels of the Methodist Church's life, communal *episkopé* is to be discerned. Moreover, there is a sense of representation at every level. Most people who serve on Church Councils are elected by the local members; most Circuit Meeting members are appointed by Church Councils; most Synod members represent Circuits; most Conference members are elected by District Synods.

23. On this point, *Called to Love and Praise* is again worth quoting:

> The Methodist understanding of authority and Church government derive from the character of Methodism as a 'connexional' Church. The interdependence which properly lies at the heart of connexionalism naturally precludes both independency and autocracy as modes of church government. Insofar as such interdependence involves submission to higher authorities (at any level), that submission is to an authority representative of the churches over which it is set. In terms of the contemporary missionary strategy of the Church, authority is vested at each level in bodies which both represent and serve the local Christian communities. [13]

24. The communal exercise of *episkopé*, especially by the Conference, but also throughout the Church's life, is characteristic of Methodism's way of exercising oversight. But what of collegial and personal *episkopé*?

2 Collegial *Episkopé*

a) The Connexion

25. The Representative Session of the Conference is, as we have seen, an example of Methodism's communal exercise of *episkopé*. The Ministerial and Diaconal Sessions, however, are better described as collegial. In each, members of the same order of ministry 'watch over' each other and take counsel together about the work of the Church, with particular regard to their own order. In former times, ministers (presbyters) valued being in the succession of 'Mr Wesley's preachers'. Collegiality was nurtured in initial training in Methodist theological colleges and sustained through an itinerant ministry that often entailed moving to a new Circuit every three years. Ministers came to value 'the brotherhood (as it then was) of the ministry' and together had a wide knowledge of the Connexion. In the last fifty years, however, changes in patterns of training, in invitation and stationing, and in the increased time ministers now spend in fewer Circuits and fewer Districts, as well

as the development of non-itinerant forms of ministry, have diminished this sense of collegiality.

26. The Methodist Diaconal Order, however, is consciously a religious order as well as an order of ministry. Its exercise of collegial oversight is found not only in the Diaconal Session of the Conference but also in the Convocation, which all deacons, diaconal probationers and student deacons are required to attend, unless a dispensation is received from the Warden. Convocation provides an opportunity not only for study, reflection and fellowship, but also for decision making and mutual accountability. Though the Warden exercises personal *episkopé* within the life of the Order, oversight is frequently seen to be exercised collegially through the Staff Team.

27. The connexional Team exists to support and encourage the Church in its ministry and mission. The Team works under the oversight of the Methodist Council and the Methodist Conference. Both its supportive rôle and its accountability to oversight indicate that the connexional Team is not intended, constitutionally, to embody collegial *episkopé*. Nevertheless, in practice the Team may be said to exercise a limited form of collegial *episkopé*. Part of the ministry of support and encouragement to the Church exercised by the Team involves considerable day to day responsibility for the Church's work. The Methodist Council further charges some connexional Team members with the responsibility of representing the Church's views, for example in areas of public policy. The exercise of such responsibilities by the connexional Team entails a kind of collegial *episkopé*, one derived ultimately from the Conference.

b)   The Districts and the Chairmen

28. Like the Ministerial Session of the Conference, the Ministerial Session of the Synod is an example of collegial *episkopé*. All members of this 'college' are expected to attend, unless given a dispensation. The Ministerial Synods play an especially important rôle of oversight in relation to probationers.

29. Later in this report, there will be some consideration of District Chairmen and the personal *episkopé* which they exercise within their Districts. It is relevant here, however, to consider three developments which have occurred in recent years with regard to the Chairmen collectively, which suggest a growing collegial exercise of *episkopé*. The first is that the Chairmen have officially become much more active in the process of stationing ministers in Circuits. They meet together to try to deal with matters of stationing with a connexional approach in mind, rather than acting as individuals, concerned mainly if not exclusively with their own Districts.

30. The second development is that the Chairmen now officially meet together at least three times a year, not only 'for the discussion of stationing issues' but also for the consideration of 'other matters of mutual concern and reflection upon the work of God in the Districts and

Connexion'.[14] The Chairmen's Meeting, however, has no specific powers, legislative or otherwise.

31. Third, at the Blackpool Conference of 1996, a statement was read out on behalf of all the Chairmen. This may be regarded as a significant development, suggesting the Chairmen acting as a 'college', part of the Conference and yet, in this instance, a distinct body within it.

c) The Circuit and the Local Church

32. There is a sense in which, within a Circuit, the Staff Meeting exercises collegial *episkopé*, as ministers, sometimes with deacons and lay workers, confer about the work of the Circuit. An extended form of this occurs when the Staff meet with the Circuit Stewards. Circuit and local church Leadership Teams could also be regarded in this way, although they may more closely approximate to the communal model.

33 The Local Preachers' Meeting, which includes ministers as well as local preachers among its members, is another example of collegial *episkopé*. Oversight is entrusted to this meeting with regard to the approval and training of those answering a call to be local preachers, to continuing local preacher development, and to matters of character, fitness and fidelity to doctrine. [15]

34 Within a local church, the collegial model of oversight is most clearly seen in the Pastoral Committee, where *episkopé* is exercised jointly, usually by consensus decision.

d) Forms of Collegiality

35. In paragraph 8 above, it was said that 'collegial oversight entails a group of people (usually ordained, and, indeed, ordained to the same order of ministry) jointly exercising *episkopé*'. That is an accurate account of how collegiality is practised in most Churches and it is found in Methodism in, for example, the Ministerial Session of the Conference and the Convocation of the Methodist Diaconal Order. There are, however, other ways in which 'colleges' are constituted in Methodism, involving not only those ordained to one particular order of ministry. Ministers, deacons, probationers and other lay people (church stewards, class leaders and pastoral visitors) may all be members of the same local church Pastoral Committee, for example.

3. **Personal *Episkopé***

36. Personal *episkopé* is widely exercised in Methodism. Ministers in local churches, Circuit Superintendents and District Chairmen are valued as pastors and leaders, and their office is recognized as conferring authority and influence. They are respected as representative persons; and this is particularly true of the President of the Conference, whose *episkopé* in other respects is limited by the short-term nature of the office.

37. It is important to the Methodist ethos that personal *episkopé* should wherever possible be exercised in a collegial or a communal context.

While pastoral care is often best given on an individual basis, matters of pastoral discipline are normally resolved by groups charged with this responsibility. A very common model of leadership is the 'minister in council' model, where the minister meets to make decisions with other ministerial or lay colleagues (the latter often elected representatives). Sometimes the exercise of personal *episkopé* means that the minister stands 'over against' the other members of the meeting, as, perhaps, when he or she is representing the interest or missionary needs of the wider Church; but the more characteristic model is leadership from within, and personal *episkopé* is characteristically exercised where the minister lives and works among the people.

a)   The Connexion

38.   The President of the Conference has considerable authority under the Methodist constitution, but this is derived authority; the President acts as the representative of the Conference. There is a sense in which the President oversees the work of the whole Connexion, but since he or she serves for only one year, this is not a sustained ministry of oversight. The President's chairing of the Methodist Council is essentially different from the 'minister-in-council' model, because of the discontinuity of the office.

39.   There is, however, continuity in the office of the Secretary of the Conference. This, combined with the unique overview of the Connexion which the rôle provides, has meant that, more at some times than at others, the Secretary has had considerable influence, if not formal authority. Some Secretaries have exercised a significant ministry of pastoral oversight. But an instinctive resistance to too much power or influence being vested in the holder of any office has ensured that this has been personal authority accorded to individual Secretaries, rather than an acceptance of the office as conferring *episkopé*.

40.   Prior to restructuring in the mid 1990s, the General Secretaries of the Divisions and their equivalents in the earlier Departments, who, with one exception, were ministers, exercised personal *episkopé*. In their relationship with the Boards, they may be thought to have approached the minister in council model (except that they did not chair Board meetings). The move towards opening most positions within the connexional Team to ordained or lay candidates has been made without addressing the serious question of how *episkopé* – whether collegial or personal in form and whether by ordained or lay people – is to be exercised at Connexional level in a way that is consonant with its exercise elsewhere. Though such sharing of responsibility is consistent with the Methodist belief in the ministry of the whole people of God, it contrasts with staff teams elsewhere in the Connexion, which usually consist largely of ministers and are usually ministerially led. Connexional Team members are less likely than staff in Circuits and Districts to understand their work in terms of personal *episkopé* either (compared with Superintendents and Chairmen) over their colleagues or (compared with circuit ministers or lay members of Circuit Leadership Teams) over the work which they are servicing.

41. The previous paragraphs suggest that personal oversight at connexional level is less clearly understood and effectively exercised than elsewhere in Methodist polity, and is not as satisfactorily provided for as are communal and collegial oversight. The Faith and Order Committee is conscious of the fact that the recently introduced connexional structures are still developing (see paragraph 27 above, for example) and does not therefore consider it appropriate to make specific recommendations about this matter at the present time. Nevertheless, the Committee believes that this is a matter of church order which it ought to keep under review; it undertakes to do so and to report further to the Conference in due course.

b) The District

42. Because, in Methodism, the geographical unit closest to a Roman Catholic or Anglican diocese is a District, the Chairman has often been perceived as exercising a rôle comparable with that of a bishop. But there are significant differences.

43. For example, a Methodist Chairman would not normally confirm, and has no authority to decide who shall be ordained, nor indeed, does he or she ordain, unless he or she is the President or is acting as the current President's deputy (a rôle almost invariably undertaken by a former President). As we have seen, the authorization of ordinations is an act of the Conference, and it is the senior representative of the Conference, or a deputy, who carries out the act. Constitutionally, the Chairman has little authority, though in practice most holders of the office enjoy considerable respect and have considerable influence.

44. The rôle of the Chairman is, in many ways, that of a circuit minister writ large. What the minister is to the congregation, the Chairman is to the District. It is a preaching, teaching and sacramental rôle. It has a large element of pastoral care; the Chairman is specifically charged with responsibility for the pastoral oversight of the ministers, deacons and probationers in the District. The Chairman also has the duty 'to exercise oversight of the character and fidelity of the ministers and ministerial probationers of the District'.[16] While the Chairman's rôle in the formal disciplinary procedures of the Church is not now as great as it once was, he or she may nevertheless have considerable personal influence and a significant informal rôle in disciplinary matters.

45. The Chairman has an important representative rôle, representing the wider Church in the local churches and the local in the wider, often shouldering connexional responsibilities, while also representing the Methodist Church in ecumenical circles and in the community at large. The Chairman is a focus of unity, and acts as a 'link-person' within a District. This involves, for example, communication, transmission of information and teaching. The Chairman may exercise a prophetic and visionary rôle, initiating new ventures in fellowship, discipleship, training and mission.

46. The nature of the rôle has developed considerably since 1957 when 'separated' Chairmen became the norm. This has happened in response

to the requirements of the Church and the expectations of the people. Though Chairmen do not normally confirm or ordain, as we have seen, their office does seem to be increasingly regarded as 'episcopal'.

c) The Circuit

47. It is often said that, in many ways, the most striking example of personal *episkopé* in British Methodism is to be found in the Circuits, in the person of the Superintendent. The Superintendent is, among the ministers of the Circuit, first among equals. He or she is responsible for the making of the preaching plan for all the churches in the Circuit. He or she has the right, seldom exercised, to preside at all official meetings. He or she is responsible for ensuring that the Church's discipline is upheld within the Circuit, and its doctrines not violated. In addition to these constitutional responsibilities, there are traditional expectations of the Superintendent's ministry: he or she is expected to exercise a preaching, pastoral, representative ministry across the Circuit, bringing leadership and co-ordination to its life.

48. The rôle of the Chairman as a minister of *episkopé* is severely qualified by Standing Orders, in favour of the Superintendent. Although 'it is the duty of the Chairman to exercise oversight of the character and fidelity of the ministers and ministerial probationers in the District', [17]

> It is the responsibility of the Chairman to strengthen the hand of the Superintendent and uphold his or her authority and rights under the Methodist constitution . . .[18]

> Each Chairman is authorized to visit officially any Circuit in the District to which he or she is invited by the Superintendent or respecting which, after consultation with the Superintendent, he or she is satisfied that his or her assistance or intervention may be necessary for the advancement of the work, the preservation of peace and order, or the execution of the connexional economy and discipline. The Chairman of the District shall not so far set aside the office and responsibility of the Superintendent as to intervene in the administration of a Circuit or to preside at any meeting for the administration of discipline or for any other circuit purposes in any Circuit except when, in special circumstances, the Synod otherwise directs, or by the invitation or with the consent of the Superintendent. Even in such circumstances, unless the Synod otherwise directs, the Superintendent shall be responsible for administering, after consultation with the Chairman and his or her own colleagues, any measure of discipline which may be deemed necessary.[19]

49. For such reasons, when the Conference of 1981 considered the possibility of introducing episcopacy into its polity, there was deep division about whether this should be done by developing the rôle of the Chairman (as the President's Council believed) or by developing the rôle of the Superintendent (as a major report before the Conference

proposed). In the event, the Conference commended the report for study, without expressing any judgment on its conclusions. [20]

50. Every minister in pastoral charge of a local church also exercises *episkopé*, supplying leadership, teaching the faith, and offering pastoral care. Commonly used terms like 'pastoral charge' and 'pastoral oversight' themselves bear witness to this fact.

d) Accountability

51. It is important to note, at the end of this brief glance at the personal *episkopé* exercised connexionally and in Districts and Circuits, that the Methodist way of doing things ensures the accountability of those who exercise oversight. Superintendents, in common with their colleagues, are subject to the processes of invitation and re-invitation. Chairmen serve for a fixed term, which is renewable by the Conference on the recommendation of the District. Officers of the Conference similarly serve for a fixed term. Personal *episkopé* can be exercised only with the consent of those among whom and with whom it is exercised. Occasionally, there may be tension between the exercise of personal *episkopé* by a minister, who by virtue of his or her ordination is a focus and representative of the calling of the whole Church, and the exercise of communal or collegial *episkopé* and decision making.

D. PREVIOUS CONSIDERATIONS OF EPISCOPACY

52. It is abundantly clear that oversight, *episkopé*, is exercised within the Connexion, and that it is exercised in personal, communal and collegial ways. For a variety of reasons, over a period of years, the Methodist Conference has considered the questions whether, when, and in what circumstances, it would be appropriate to move beyond the recognition that *episkopé* is exercised within the Connexion to the introduction of **episcopacy**. The 1998 report (see paragraph 2 above) quoted extensively from the many statements about episcopacy which had been made in Methodist documents since the time of Methodist union. It is neither necessary nor desirable to reproduce all those quotations here, but it may well be helpful to summarize them as follows.

   a) The Conference has recognized that *episkopé* is already exercised within the life of the Methodist Church.

   b) The Conference has asserted its view that episcopacy is not essential to the existence or apostolicity of the Church, but has also expressed its belief that 'the coming great Church will be congregational, presbyteral, and episcopal in its life and order'.

   c) The Conference has declared that the acceptance of the 'historic episcopate' would not violate the Methodist doctrinal standards.

   d) In the context of proposals towards closer unity, the Conference has on several occasions indicated its willingness to embrace episcopacy, while insisting that Methodists should have no less freedom of interpretation than Anglicans enjoy in respect of the 'historic episcopate'.

E. MODELS OF THE EPISCOPATE FROM THE WORLD-WIDE CHURCH

53. The 1998 Conference, in commissioning the present report, directed that it should 'explore models of the episcopate from the world-wide Church'. This section of the report sketches out a selection of such models, beginning with Churches from the Methodist tradition, then in the Anglican, Roman Catholic and Moravian traditions. The concluding paragraphs of the section consider the place of episcopacy within a number of united Churches and important ecumenical agreements.

1. The United Methodist Church

54. The United Methodist Church (a global Church based in the United States of America) is an example of a Methodist Church in which *episkopé* is exercised by bishops. Although John Wesley disapproved of Thomas Coke and Francis Asbury being called 'bishops', he 'appointed' them (or 'ordained' them, as he sometimes wrote) to superintend the work in America. Within Wesley's own lifetime, the term 'bishop' was in use in American Methodism. The bishops of the United Methodist Church are elected by a Jurisdictional or Central Conference and usually consecrated at a session of the same Conference. They are regarded as elders (presbyters) exercising a particular office, rather than members of a distinct order of ministry, though on retirement they are eligible to attend the Council of Bishops without voting rights. It is their responsibility to lead and oversee 'the spiritual and temporal affairs of the United Methodist Church, and particularly to lead the Church in its mission and service to the world',[21] and to transmit, teach and proclaim the apostolic faith. The bishops appoint district superintendents, consecrate bishops and ordain elders and deacons.

55. The United Methodist Church places great emphasis on the collegiality of bishops:

> Bishops, although elected by Jurisdictional or Central Conferences, are elected general superintendents of the whole Church. As all ordained ministers are first elected into membership of an Annual Conference and subsequently appointed to pastoral charges, so bishops become through their election members first of the Council of Bishops before they are subsequently assigned to areas of service.[22]

> The Council of Bishops is thus the collegial expression of episcopal leadership in the Church and through the Church into the world. The Church expects the Council of Bishops to speak to the Church and from the Church to the world, and to give leadership in the quest for Christian unity . . .[23]

56. *Episkopé* is exercised in the United Methodist Church not only by bishops, but also by district superintendents. The rôle of the latter is largely pastoral. The Book of Discipline indicates that they are to give pastoral support and supervision to the clergy of the district and encourage their personal, spiritual and professional growth. They are to enable programmes that may assist local churches to build and extend

their ministry and mission with their people and to the community. They are also to participate with the bishops in the appointment-making process and to assist the bishop in the administration of the Annual Conference.[24] There is strong emphasis on the bishops and district superintendents as leaders in mission:

> The task of superintending the United Methodist Church resides in the office of the bishop and extends to the district superintendent . . . The purpose of superintending is to equip the Church in its disciple-making ministry. [25]

57. It should be noted that the United Methodist Church does not claim that its bishops stand within the 'historic succession'.

2. The Methodist Church of Southern Africa and the Methodist Church in Portugal.

58. The Methodist Church of Southern Africa (MCSA) and the Methodist Church in Portugal (IEMP) both provide examples of Methodist Churches that have recently moved from non-episcopal to episcopal forms of Church life.

59. The MCSA began as an overseas District of the British Methodist Church. After becoming autonomous, it continued to be structured along similar lines to British Methodism. In the 1980s discussion about whether to retitle MCSA's District Chairmen 'bishops' gathered pace. In ecumenical contexts, and in relation to the media and political authorities, some argued, the term 'District Chairman' did not achieve sufficient recognition. Amongst opponents of the proposed change there were suspicions about the 'trappings' of episcopal office and serious anxiety about an erosion of the democratic accountability of Church leaders if the Church decided to have bishops. In due course the Conference of the MCSA decided to change the title of District Chairmen to 'Bishop'. Greater autonomy has been given to Districts. The Annual Conference has become a triennial Conference. Between Conferences a Connexional Executive oversees the Church; nearly half of its forty members are Bishops.

60. For the first century and a quarter of its existence the Methodist Church in Portugal was also an Overseas District of the British Methodist Conference. In 1996 the 'Iglesia Evangelica Metodista Portuguesa' became an autonomous Church. It chose to entitle the leader of the Church 'Bishop'. *The Basic Doctrines and Statutes of the IEMP* affirm that, for reasons of 'order, discipline and efficiency', the IEMP sets aside by ordination a diaconal ministry and a ministry of Word and Sacrament. They continue:

> The Episcopate of the IEMP is not a ministerial order different from, or hierarchically superior to, the Presbyteral order, but an office within that order. Its functions comprise a pastoral ministry, which embraces the whole Church and includes the pastoral care of all the other presbyters, and the preservation and elucidation of the faith. The Episcopate is a symbol of

Church unity and the Bishop is primarily responsible for the official representation of the Church on all occasions and in all places where such representation is required.[26]

3. British Anglican Churches

61. For British Methodists, considerations of episcopacy notably take place in the context of their experience of it in the three churches of the Anglican Communion in Wales, Scotland and England. At the present time, Methodist representatives are participating in important ecumenical conversations in England, Scotland and Wales, each of which involves an Anglican Church and in each of which, therefore, episcopacy is an issue to be addressed.

62. *Sharing in the Apostolic Communion*, a report of the Anglican-Methodist International Commission, helpfully sets out the current Anglican understanding of the 'historic episcopate':

> Within Anglicanism, the historic episcopate denotes the continuity of oversight in the Church through the ages from the earliest days, expressed in a personal episcopal ministry, the intention of which is to safeguard, transmit, and restate in every generation the apostolic faith delivered once for all to the saints. It is not the only way by which the apostolic faith is safeguarded and transmitted, nor is it exercised apart from the Church as a whole. It is exercised within the Church, recalling the people of God to their apostolic vocation. It is exercised in an interplay with the whole people of God, in which their reception of that ministry is a crucial element . . . It is a personal episcopal ministry, but always exercised collegially (i.e. together with other bishops, and with the clergy within each diocese), and also communally (i.e. together with the laity and clergy in synod, convention or council).[27]

63. It is not to be assumed, however, that because the Church of England, the Episcopal Church of Scotland and the Church in Wales are all members of the Anglican Communion, the same model of episcopacy is to be found in all of them. Episcopacy may be exercised with different 'styles' and may 'feel' different in different contexts. For example, the episcopal office in the Church of England, which is the Established Church in that country, carries with it certain differences of function and perhaps status from those obtaining in the non-established Anglican churches in Scotland and Wales. Bishops of the Church of England are nominated by the Church, but, unlike their counterparts in Wales and Scotland, appointed by the Crown.

a) The Church of England

64. Within the Church of England, the bishop in his diocese is the chief pastor and principal minister. He ordains priests and deacons. He confirms. His responsibilities include 'conducting, ordering, controlling and authorising all services . . .' and 'of granting a faculty or licence for all alterations, removals, or repairs to the walls, fabric, ornaments or

furniture . . .'[28] He institutes clergy to vacant benefices. He may well perform a function in affairs of state as a member of the House of Lords. He represents the whole Church in and to his diocese, and his diocese in and to the councils of the Church. 'He is thus a living representative of the unity and universality of the Church.'[29] With his fellow bishops he has the responsibility to guard the Church against erroneous teaching.

65. But the concept of a single bishop in a diocese has been modified. There are suffragan bishops or area bishops, who exercise some of the functions of the diocesan bishop, sometimes in clearly-defined sections of a diocese, sometimes throughout a diocese. They act under delegation from their diocesan bishops. There are now the Provincial Episcopal Visitors, recently consecrated as bishops to provide ministry and pastoral care to those within the Church of England who are opposed to the ordination of women and who do not feel able to accept sacramental ministry and pastoral care from diocesan or suffragan bishops who have ordained women to the priesthood. Numerous reports to the General Synod, on matters related to the exercise of episcopacy, make it abundantly clear, not only that practical changes have occurred, but also that there is a developing understanding of what episcopacy means.

66. The Church of England describes itself as 'episcopally led and synodically governed'.[30] The rôle of the bishops within that synodical government appears to be highly significant. The Synodical Government Measure of 1969 provided for the formation of the General Synod and enabled 'the laity to take their place alongside the clergy in the Councils of the Church'. Diocesan Synods also now exist and are designed to be democratically representative. The bishop presides at the Synod, though others may do so at the bishop's invitation.

67. The General Synod is presided over by the two Archbishops. Within it, the House of Bishops exercises a certain amount of collegial power. Matters of doctrine, liturgy, ceremonial and the administration of the sacraments go before the House of Bishops before going to the Synod and then are referred back for final approval, thus reflecting the bishops' continuing authority over matters of oversight and the guardianship of faith and order. On occasion the House of Bishops is responsible for bringing before the Synod legislation which is largely of its own (the House of Bishops') making, for example, the Episcopal Ministry Act of Synod 1993 which provided for extended episcopal oversight, including Provincial Episcopal Visitors.

b) The Scottish Episcopal Church and the Church in Wales

68. The 'feel' of Anglicanism in Scotland and Wales is significantly different from that in England. This may in part result from the fact that the Anglican Churches of Scotland and Wales are not established. Furthermore, because there are comparatively few bishops (six in Wales and seven in Scotland) and because the churches themselves are relatively small, both episcopal collegiality and a sense of closeness between bishop, clergy and people are perhaps more evident than in the Church of England. Bishops are individually involved in a wider range of national church activities than is the case in England.

69. In the Interim Report of the Scottish Church Initiative for Union, episcopal ministry in the Scottish Episcopal Church is described in the following terms:

> Paramount in the personal dimension of this ministry of oversight is the need for pastoral care and leadership in mission in a way that brings cohesion . . . In the Scottish Episcopal Church bishops serve in collaborative ministry with each other, other ministers and the councils of the Church at all levels. For the discharge of their duties they are answerable to the Church. They have a constitutionally defined rôle alongside others in the governance of the Church.[31]

70. The Church in Wales, like the Methodist Church, is one of the Covenanted Churches which are exploring the possibility of an 'ecumenical bishop'. Though the outcome of this exploration cannot at present be known, the engagement in it of the Church in Wales illustrates a willingness (expressed in the Welsh Anglican/Methodist talks of 1965) 'to look forward to what episcopacy may become, as we live together'. In Scotland too there is a recognition that episcopacy is evolving.

71. The Episcopal Church of Scotland, the Church in Wales and the Church of England have all experienced developments in their understandings and styles of episcopacy. Especially in ecumenical conversations, they have revealed an openness to further developments. In the context of a discussion of 'the Apostolicity of the Church and Ministry', the report of the Conversations between the British and Irish Anglican Churches and the French Lutheran Churches, declared that 'all our churches are churches in change . . . Anglicans, for example, are presently concerned to find the right balance between synodical government and episcopal oversight.' [32]

4. The Roman Catholic Church

72. The Roman Catholic Church has a hierarchical understanding of episcopacy. Episcopal consecration confers 'the fullness of the sacrament of orders . . . the apex of the sacred ministry'.[33] The bishops are the successors of the apostles. They care for the flock of Christ by governing it and teaching it.[34] Each 'individual bishop . . . is the visible principle and foundation of unity in his particular church'.[35] Bishops 'have the sacred right and the duty before the Lord to make laws for their subjects, to pass judgement on them, and to moderate everything pertaining to the ordering of worship . . .'[36] The Second Vatican Council stressed the collegiality of the episcopate, referring to the ecumenical councils held through the centuries. 'But the college or body of bishops has no authority unless it is simultaneously conceived of in terms of its head, the Roman Pontiff, Peter's successor . . .'[37] who 'has full, supreme, and universal power over the Church'.[38] Thus, bishops have considerable authority and power within their dioceses, but it is always exercised under the higher authority of the Pope. Diocesan bishops are

sometimes assisted by Auxiliary bishops who act under their authority. Bishops ordain and usually confirm, though this latter responsibility is sometimes delegated to presbyters.

73. Since the Second Vatican Council, Roman Catholic understanding of episcopacy has advanced in parallel with the recovery of the understanding of the Church as *koinonia* (fellowship, communion), and bishops are seen as leaders of their local churches and active collaborators with the Pope, rather than simply as his agents. It is also true that much modern Roman Catholic theology emphasizes the duty of bishops to listen to and represent their local churches. Yet the Roman Catholic model of episcopacy remains essentially hierarchical and the bishops' collegiality is based on the principle of 'hierarchical communion' with the Pope, juridically enforced.

5. The Moravian Church

74. The Moravian Church, which profoundly influenced early Methodism, is an example of an episcopal church, in the historic succession, in which Church-governmental and administrative functions are not necessarily linked to the office of a bishop. The bishop is seen as 'a living symbol of the continuity of the Church's ministry'. His primary responsibility is spiritual; he has a special duty to intercede for the Church; he is a pastor to the pastors; he should visit congregations in order to deepen their spiritual life and his opinion should be sought in matters of doctrine and practice. The Bishop represents the whole Church in the act of ordination, but ordains only on the authority of a Provincial Board or Synod. [39]

6. The Church of South India

75. The twentieth century has witnessed a number of important schemes for Christian unity and some significant ecumenical agreements. Whenever episcopally-ordered Churches (especially those which claim the historic episcopate) have been involved, episcopacy has been an issue to be addressed.

76. The Church of South India (CSI) is an example of a United Church into which Methodists entered, and which involved acceptance by Methodists and other non-episcopal churches not only of an episcopal Church structure, but also of the historic episcopate.

77. Acceptance of the historic episcopate within the CSI was a much debated issue by the participating Churches in advance of Union. Congregationalists, Methodists, Presbyterians and other Reformed Church representatives agreed to lay aside their historic reservations about episcopacy for the sake of Union. Methodist missionaries from Britain, who originated mainly in the Wesleyan tradition, self-consciously provided a bridge between Anglicans and the 'Free Churches' on this issue. To achieve Church Union compromise was necessary, not least on episcopacy. The CSI Constitution, written before Union, deliberately did not include the expression of a particular understanding of episcopacy.

7. The Uniting Church of Australia

78. By contrast with the CSI, the Uniting Church of Australia is an example of a uniting Church that considered accepting the historic episcopate, but resolved for the time being not to do so.

79. The Uniting Church of Australia brings together Congregational, Presbyterian and Methodist traditions. In the earliest stages Anglicans were also involved. *The Second Report of the Joint Commission on Church Union* looked in detail at episcopacy and recommended accepting the sign of the historic episcopate on the basis that the office of bishop was present in the Church from the earliest times. It was recommended that the sign be recovered from the Church of South India, because the Joint Commission understood that Bishops in the CSI avoided 'prelatical episcopacy'. The pattern of 'bishop in presbytery', the Report suggested, might find wide acceptance in the proposed Uniting Church in Australia. Ultimately, Church Union proceeded along non-episcopal lines, and without Anglican participation.

8. Episcopacy in the Leuenberg, Meissen, Porvoo and Reuilly Ecumenical Agreements

80. The Leuenberg Agreement is an ecumenical accord between Churches of the Lutheran and Reformed traditions. Most of the Methodist Churches of Europe, including the British Methodist Church, have accepted it and are members of the Leuenberg Fellowship of Churches. The Meissen Agreement is between the Church of England and the Evangelical Church in Germany (a federation of Churches from Lutheran, Reformed and United Church traditions). The Porvoo Common Statement marks an agreement between the British and Irish Anglican Churches and the Nordic and Baltic Lutheran Churches. The Reuilly Common Statement resulted from conversations between the British and Irish Anglican Churches and the French Lutheran and Reformed Churches. Because British Methodists are part of Leuenberg, but not of Meissen and Porvoo, the Leuenberg Agreement is of particular interest.

81. The Leuenberg Agreement allows for areas of doctrinal disagreement between member Churches. It provides for church fellowship, but does not seek formal church union. In the original Agreement little is said about understandings of ministry, and nothing specifically of episcopacy. Yet the Agreement does declare 'mutual recognition of ordination and the freedom to provide for inter-celebration at the Lord's Supper'.

82. In a subsequent document, *Sacraments, Ministry, Ordination*, participating Churches state a set of theses on Ministry, which include the following:

> In ecumenical discussion there is . . . increasing talk of a 'service of *episkopé*'. In the New Testament there is no clearly recognizable difference between presbyters and *episcopoi*. Certainly not all congregations had *episcopoi*. Nevertheless the 'historic episcopate' did develop in the tradition.[40]

83. In Reformed churches, it adds, presbyters have exercised a service of *episkopé*, and in the Lutheran Churches there is an episcopal ministry. But, despite different practices, 'the Churches of the Reformation are unanimous that they do not regard the churches as founded on the office of bishop. They understand the 'service of *episkopé*' exclusively as a service to the unity of the church, not as an office (*Amt*) over the church, but as a service (*Dienst*) in the church.'[41]

84. The German churches, which are signatories to the Leuenberg Agreement, are also part of the Meissen Agreement. In Meissen, the crucial paragraph is #16. This spells out a disagreement at the heart of the Meissen Agreement:

> Lutheran, Reformed and United Churches, though being increasingly prepared to appreciate episcopal succession 'as a sign of the apostolicity of the life of the whole Church' hold that this particular form of *episkopé* should not become a necessary condition for 'full, visible unity'. The Anglican understanding of full, visible unity includes the historic episcopate and full interchangeability of ministers. Because of this remaining difference our mutual recognition of one another's ministries does not result yet in the full interchangeability of ministers.[42]

85. In Porvoo, even this obstacle is absent, and consequently the Nordic and Baltic Churches, which have the historic episcopate, are in the same degree of fellowship with the Anglican Churches of the British Isles as Provinces of the Anglican Communion outside the British Isles.

86. The Reuilly Common Statement was published as recently as 1999. It includes the following sentences:

> Anglicans believe that the historic episcopate is a sign of the apostolicity of the whole Church . . . Anglicans hold that the full visible unity of the Church includes the historic episcopal succession . . . Lutherans and Reformed also believe that their ministries are in apostolic succession. In their ordination rites they emphasize the continuity of the Church and its ministry. They can recognize in the historic episcopal succession a sign of the apostolicity of the Church. They do not, however, consider it a necessary condition for full visible unity . . . Anglicans increasingly recognize that a continuity in apostolic faith, worship and mission has been preserved in churches which have not retained the historic episcopal succession. However, Anglicans commend the use of the sign to signify: God's promise to be with the Church; God's call to fidelity and to unity; and a commission to realize more fully the permanent characteristics of the Church of the apostles. Because of this remaining difference . . . our mutual recognition of one another's ministries does not yet result in the full interchangeability of ordained ministers.[43]

9. A Development in the United States of America

87. The *Concordat of Agreement* between the Episcopal (Anglican) Church of the United States of America and the Evangelical Lutheran Church in America, which currently has bishops who are not in the 'historic succession', offers a model for reconciliation between a Church claiming the historic episcopate and one not claiming it. The *Concordat*, which has been approved by the Lutheran Church and awaits approval by the Episcopal Church, will, when fully ratified, enable full interchangeability of ministries and a degree of mutual consultation and accountability. To enable this to happen, the Episcopal Church will temporarily suspend the restriction that no one shall exercise ministry as a bishop, priest or deacon who has not been ordained within the historic episcopate.[44] The two churches will acknowledge each others' ministries as 'given by God . . . in the service of God's people'.[45] The Episcopalians will acknowledge that the historic episcopate is not 'necessary for salvation or for the recognition of another Church as a Church'.[46] The two churches will remain free to keep their existing links of communion with other churches, whether episcopal or non-episcopal. The Lutherans will receive the sign of the historical succession through the future consecration of bishops by others who stand in that succession, though they are not thereby required to affirm that such episcopacy is necessary for the unity of the Church.[47]

10. The World Church

88. The development of British Methodist understanding of *episkopé* and of episcopacy does not take place in isolation from the World Church. The British Methodist Church is committed to an enriching and challenging pattern of relationships with partner Churches from Methodist and other traditions. From the brief sketches above, it is clear that British Methodism's partners in the World Church have explored very similar questions to those addressed in the present report. They have come to a wide range of conclusions. Some have continued without bishops; some have introduced bishops, but not within the historic episcopate; yet others have accepted the historic episcopate.

F. *EPISKOPÉ*, EPISCOPACY AND BRITISH METHODISM

89. The 1998 Conference directed the Faith and Order Committee to offer 'guidelines on issues of oversight, including those concerning bishops, which may guide Methodist representatives in ecumenical conversations and assist the development of our own structures'.

90. It is clear to the Faith and Order Committee that the issue is not simply one of terminology. The expression 'District Chairman' has come to be regarded by many people as unsatisfactory for two reasons. First, it violates the principle, strongly endorsed by the Conference, of the use of inclusive language. Second, it is largely unintelligible to the wider community. From time to time, and as recently as 1998, the suggestion has been made that these difficulties could be overcome if the

'Chairmen' were called 'Bishops'. But, while it is clear that 'District Chairman' is not a satisfactory term, the Faith and Order Committee believes that the straight substitution of the term 'bishop' is not an acceptable solution to the difficulty, for the following reasons.

91. First, the proposal to entitle Chairmen 'bishops' takes it for granted that the Chairmen would be the obvious people to be so named. The 1981 report (see paragraph 49 above) took a different view. A change of name should not take place without a serious study of the implications of such a change, some of which are addressed in paragraphs 102 – 109 below.

92. Second, although the Faith and Order Committee does not intend to pass any judgment on Methodist Churches in other parts of the world which have adopted the title 'bishop', the Committee believes that the ecumenical context which obtains in the British Isles renders such a course inappropriate for British Methodism. Only confusion would result if a title extensively used throughout the Christian world, but not previously used in British Methodism, were suddenly adopted and invested with a distinctive meaning, which took no account of the traditional rôle of a bishop, as described in paragraph 94 below. Such a procedure would be likely to hinder rather than to advance the cause of Christian unity, especially in relation to Churches which place great emphasis upon the historic episcopate.

93. This is not to say that there is only one way in which episcopacy can be understood. Section E above briefly illustrated the diversity which presently exists. Nevertheless, there are common features in the picture that emerges from that section. They are as follows.

94. **It is generally agreed, in episcopal churches, that bishops are to exercise oversight, both within their particular areas of responsibility and in the wider Church. Bishops exercise their oversight both individually and collegially, and in many episcopal churches play a leading rôle, alongside presbyters, deacons and lay people, in church government. They have responsibility for the transmission and safeguarding of the apostolic faith, for providing for the administering of the sacraments, and for leadership in the Church's mission. They ordain presbyters and deacons. Their prophetic rôle includes the responsibility to represent the concerns of the wider Church to their dioceses, as they listen to and share with others the insights and witness of their own local churches.**

95. These common features of episcopacy, as it is generally understood among episcopal churches, would have to be taken seriously by British Methodism if the introduction of a form of episcopacy to Methodism were to contribute to, rather than to impede, progress towards unity.

96. The report adopted by the 1998 Conference, having surveyed the discussion of episcopacy in British Methodism from 1937 onwards, noted that, while British Methodism does not regard episcopacy as being an essential element of Church order, the Conference has expressed its

willingness to embrace the historic episcopate in order to further the cause of Christian unity.

97. In view of the significance which many churches attach to the historic episcopate, it would be misguided to introduce a form of episcopacy into British Methodism which would not be recognized by other churches as being within the historic episcopate. The recent *Concordat* of the Evangelical Lutherans and Episcopalians in the United States of America (see paragraph 87 above) illustrates the point that for significant progress to be made towards the reconciliation of ministries, the question of the 'historic succession' cannot be evaded. If Methodism is to advance towards unity with episcopally ordered churches in the historic succession, then at some stage, it must embrace episcopacy in that succession. This has been acknowledged in the past, as, for example, when, in its response to *Baptism, Eucharist and Ministry*, the Conference of 1985 declared:

> . . . we await the occasion when it would be appropriate 'to recover the sign of the episcopal succession'.[48]

98. The Conference of 1978 expressed its belief that episcopacy would be one of the characteristics of 'the coming great Church'. It is unrealistic to imagine that the considerable majority of Christians whose churches are episcopally ordered would be willing to give up a sign of apostolicity which they cherish, and indeed it would be unreasonable to expect them to do so. It would be characteristic of Methodism to be open to the possibility that something that had not previously been a feature of Methodist life might contribute to it and enrich it.

99. Hitherto, the Conference has taken the view that such a momentous step should be taken only in the context of a unity scheme, rather than as an independent denominational act. The time and energy that would be involved in doing the latter would be considerable, and could be justified only if it were clear that the introduction of episcopacy to Methodism would either significantly enhance the way in which *episkopé* is exercised among us or that it would help to bring the unity of the Church closer. Since *episkopé* is already exercised throughout the Methodist Church's life (though imperfectly), and since discussions of various sorts are currently underway with the Anglican churches of England, Scotland and Wales, in which episcopacy is one of the issues under discussion, it would be unwise for the Methodist Church to act independently at the present time.

100. The judgment of the Faith and Order Committee is, therefore, that it would be helpful for the Conference to affirm its willingness to embrace episcopacy in the context of a unity scheme or as a significant step to bring the unity of the Church closer, but that the Conference should not seek to develop its own form of episcopacy outside that context. The Committee hopes that the preceding sentence will be read, not as a turning away from considerations of episcopacy, but rather as a call to engage seriously with partner churches in the search for a form of episcopacy which all can own and cherish.

101. If conversations with a church or churches within the historic episcopate were to lead to a scheme for full visible unity, such a scheme would clearly need to set out a proposal for the way in which episcopal ministry would be exercised in the united Church. It could be, however, that conversations might result in a scheme for much closer relationships and partnerships, including perhaps reconciliation and interchangeability of ministries, while the churches continued to exist as separate entities. If the introduction of the historic episcopate to those churches which previously lacked it were part of such proposals, it would clearly be helpful for the Methodist Church to have a considered answer to the many questions which would need to be addressed before episcopacy could be introduced. These are set out in paragraphs 102 to 109 below.

102. First, who would become bishops? In previous considerations of this question, British Methodism has looked at three possibilities. The 1981 report claimed that

> As the bishop is a focus of oversight and unity in the church, it would be natural for the President to be a bishop. Moreover, he engages in the kind of ministry traditionally associated with bishops (for example, in ordaining and in presiding over the Conference to which oversight of doctrine is committed). However to have only the President as bishop would be to remove the bishop from the close contact with the local church and the local minister which is generally seen as one of the most valuable parts of his ministry. Moreover the presence of perhaps ten or a dozen Past Presidents engaged in a ministry that is not necessarily one which focusses oversight and unity would severely distort the rôle of a bishop in the church . . . If the President is to be a bishop, which we judge to be right, then it is important that the more usual expression of episcopacy be elsewhere. [49]

103. Those observations from the 1981 report, with which the Faith and Order Committee concurs, leave two possibilities for 'the more usual expression of episcopacy': the District Chairmen and the Circuit Superintendents. If the latter became bishops, this would presumably require the formation of fewer and much larger Circuits, since it would not be easy for over 300 bishops to relate to the bishops of other churches, or for that matter to each other. What, in these circumstances, would become of the Chairman's rôle? On the other hand, if the Chairmen rather than the Superintendents became bishops, how would their rôle and their constitutional responsibilities, and those of Superintendents, as set out in the Deed of Union and Standing Orders, need to be amended in order that appropriate oversight might be exercised?

104. Second, there is the matter of the relationship between the bishops on the one hand and the Conference and its President on the other. As we have seen, *episkopé* is exercised corporately by the Conference and, derivatively, by individuals, as well as collegially. There is no reason to suppose that the introduction of bishops would detract from the authority

of the Conference, since bishops would exercise oversight under the authority of the Conference and be accountable to it.

105. The relationship between the bishops and the President (if the latter were not a bishop) would, however, raise difficulties. The latter, or his or her deputy, acts on behalf of the Conference at ordinations, the vast majority of which take place during the period when the Conference is meeting and within easy reach of the Conference venue. This practice is derived from, and has helped to maintain, the connexionalism that is such an important part of Methodism. Yet it is a universally recognized feature of episcopacy that bishops ordain and such ordinations usually take place within the diocese where those to be ordained serve. It would be extraordinary to have Methodist bishops who did not ordain, and the introduction of bishops would therefore be bound to involve some changes in the way in which Methodist ordinations are organized. Yet it ought to be possible to devise some means whereby bishops, alongside the President or a deputy, could play a leading rôle in ordinations, thus preserving the connexional principle while introducing episcopal ordination. For example, if the Chairmen became bishops, ordinations could take place at the Conference for groups of three or four Districts. The President or a deputy would preside at the services. Each bishop, with the President, could ordain the candidates from his or her District. It would be less easy to see how this problem might be resolved if the Superintendents were to become bishops.

106. There are other issues, however, about the relationship between the President and Methodist bishops. The former fulfils many rôles during the presidential year, for example in visits to Districts and to some extent in matters of discipline, which might be thought to be 'episcopal' rôles. If Chairmen or Superintendents became bishops, some re-evaluation of presidential responsibilities would be necessary.

107. Third, another common feature of episcopal churches is the concept of bishops acting collegially. Reference has already been made to the Church of England's House of Bishops and to the United Methodist Church, in whose understanding 'the Council of Bishops is the collegial expression of episcopal leadership'. At present, British Methodism has no equivalent. The District Chairmen meet together regularly, but they do not have authority to speak or act corporately on behalf of or to the Connexion. Nevertheless, as has already been pointed out, there have been developments in the way in which Chairmen operate collegially, and the introduction of bishops would require closer examination of the collegial rôle that they might properly exercise.

108. Fourth, careful consideration should be given to how episcopacy relates to county, regional and national structures and to how 'subsidiarity' may develop in the way in which authority is exercised within the Church. Would it be appropriate to have more than one type of episcopal area (for example, metropolitan districts, rural areas, small town) some with 'separated' and some with 'non-separated' bishops?

109. Fifth, there is the question of the means whereby British Methodism should receive the historic episcopate. In the context of conversations

involving British Anglicans, it would clearly be appropriate for them to be involved in the first Methodist episcopal ordinations. But it would also be appropriate for the Methodist Church to receive the sign from a church or churches within the historic episcopate with which it is already in communion. The Church of South India is an obvious example.

110. The questions raised in paragraphs 102 to 109 above need to be addressed in the context of Methodism's experience of the exercise of *episkopé*, communally, collegially and personally, as described in part C of this report, and in the light of the guidelines in part H. The Faith and Order Committee believes that widespread discussion of these questions is desirable in order to discover how a Methodist episcopate would operate and therefore offers the third recommendation in part G and Resolution 3 to enable such a process.

G. RECOMMENDATIONS

111. The Faith and Order Committee recommends that the Conference, while taking no immediate steps to introduce episcopacy into Methodist polity, should affirm its willingness to do so in the context of appropriate ecumenical developments, on the basis of the Guidelines set out in section H below.

112. The Committee further recommends that these Guidelines be adopted by the Conference in order (a) to assist Methodist representatives in ecumenical conversations faithfully to convey to others the mind of the Conference and (b) to assist in the development of our own structures.

113. Finally, the Committee recommends that this report be commended to the Methodist people for discussion, and that they be invited to comment on the issues raised in paragraphs 89 – 109 above.

H. GUIDELINES

114. The Faith and Order Committee proposes that the following Guidelines be adopted as a summary statement of the Methodist Church's position on *episkopé* and episcopacy.

1. The Methodist Church recognizes that *episkopé* is exercised within its life in communal, collegial and personal ways.

    a. The Methodist Church values communal *episkopé*, exercised by representative bodies throughout the Church's life.

    The Conference and the District Synod, in their representative sessions, Circuit Meetings and Church Councils are examples of the exercise of communal *episkopé*.

    b. The Methodist Church values collegial *episkopé*, and its tradition of expressing collegiality, not only among members of the same order of ministry, but also among lay persons and ordained persons.

Examples of such collegiality include the Ministerial Session of the Conference, which is made up of ministers, and Local Preachers Meetings and local church Pastoral Committees, where collegial oversight is shared by ordained and lay persons.

c. **The Methodist Church values personal *episkopé* in every part of the Church's life, but believes that such *episkopé* should be exercised within a collegial or communal context.**

It is important that personal *episkopé* be allowed for within connexional structures in ways consonant with its exercise in Circuits and Districts. Because the *episkopé* exercised by individuals within the life of the Methodist Church is derived or representative oversight, it is important that those who exercise personal *episkopé* remain accountable to the wider Church. It must be recognized that the need to be accountable and the need to maintain proper confidentiality may sometimes be in conflict.

2. **The Methodist Church is a connexional Church and all *episkopé* should be exercised within this context. In the development of any structures, due consideration should be given to their impact upon the life of the whole Church. There is a proper balance to be maintained between, for example, Circuit and District or District and Connexion.**

While recognizing the value of a diocesan model, the Methodist Church would be uneasy about the development of any models of personal *episkopé* which isolated Districts from the whole Church.

3. **The Methodist Church began as a missionary movement and continues to have mission at its heart. Methodists believe that a key function of *episkopé* is to enable and encourage the Church's participation in God's mission.**

The missionary imperative was an important consideration in the introduction of 'separated' Chairmen. The experience of some Methodist Churches, including the United Methodist Church, which have adopted episcopal systems of oversight provides encouraging precedents for expressions of *episkopé* that are mission-led.

4. **In the furtherance of the search for the visible unity of Christ's Church, the Methodist Church would willingly receive the sign of episcopal succession on the understanding that ecumenical partners sharing this sign with the Methodist Church (a) acknowledge that the latter has been and is part of the one holy catholic and apostolic Church and (b) accept that different interpretations of the precise significance of the sign exist.**

As to (a), this was something that the Conference asked of the Church of England in 1955 as the 'Conversations' began. Many people in our partner churches would themselves be anxious to ensure that nothing done in the uniting of ministries should imply that previous ministries were invalid or inauthentic.

As to (b), Methodism has previously insisted that there should be freedom of interpretation as to the significance of the historic episcopate. The concept that episcopacy is a 'sign but not a guarantee of the apostolicity of the Church' may be widely acceptable as a testimony to its symbolic witness to links across time, while testifying too to the obvious truth that bishops are not automatically and invariably wise or faithful.

5. **The Methodist Church, in contemplating the possibility of receiving the sign of the historic episcopal succession, expects to engage in dialogue with its sister Churches to clarify as thoroughly as possible the nature and benefits of this gift.**

In considering the introduction of the historic succession to Methodism in the sort of circumstances outlined in Guideline 2, the Methodist Church recognizes the need to explore its potential for complementing and enriching the Methodist Church's present experience of *episkopé* and for enhancing Methodism's sense of communion within the one holy catholic and apostolic Church.

6. **The Methodist Church would be unable to receive the sign of episcopal succession in a context which would involve a repudiation of what the Methodist Church believed itself to have received from God.**

An obvious and important example of what is meant by this Guideline is the ministry of women. Since women were ordained to the presbyterate in the Methodist Church, every office for which male ministers are eligible has been open also to women. In its preliminary consideration of the scheme for an Ecumenical Bishop in Wales, the Conference was extremely concerned by the statement that the first such bishop would necessarily be male, and it gave its approval for further work to be done on the scheme on the understanding that serious efforts would be made in the ongoing discussions to ensure that such a restriction should not obtain in relation to any subsequent appointment.

7. **The Methodist Church, in receiving the sign of episcopal succession, would insist that all ministries, including those of oversight, are exercised <u>within</u> the ministry of the whole people of God and at its service, rather than in isolation from it and in supremacy over it.**

In earlier conversations, the Methodist Church has emphasized the value which it would place on the pastoral office of bishops, and on bishops having leadership responsibilities for mission and a representative rôle in community affairs. The view has been expressed that they should know and be known at many levels, and that they should exercise authority with gentleness and be humble servants of Christ.

As the survey of styles of *episkopé* and of episcopacy indicated, Methodists should not fear that the adoption of episcopacy would, of necessity, involve the adoption of a hierarchical model. Increasingly, in episcopally ordered churches, emphasis has been placed on the pastoral, teaching and missionary rôles of the bishop. As *Commitment to Mission and Unity* insists:

>The office [of a bishop] is relational in character and must be exercised in, with and among the community which it is called to serve. The office should not be so overburdened with bureaucratic demands that bishops are prevented from being alongside their people, or that their collegiality with their fellow bishops, presbyters and deacons is diminished. It is a ministry of service which requires an appropriate lifestyle and pastoral demeanour.[50]

RESOLUTIONS

7/1. The Conference adopts the Guidelines set out in this report as a summary statement of its position on *episkopé* and episcopacy.

7/2. The Conference affirms its willingness in principle to receive the sign of episcopacy on the basis of the Guidelines set out in this report.

7/3. The Conference receives the report and commends it to the Methodist Youth Conference, the Districts, Circuits and local churches for discussion.

7/4. The Conference invites the Methodist Youth Conference, the Districts, Circuits, local churches and individual Methodists to send comments on paragraphs 89 to 109 to the Secretary of the Faith and Order Committee not later than 31 December 2001, and directs the Faith and Order Committee to report to the Conference of 2002 on the comments received.

REFERENCES

1. *Sharing in the Apostolic Communion*, a Report of the Anglican-Methodist International Commission to the World Methodist Council and the Lambeth Conference, 1996, pp.30f
2. *Baptism, Eucharist and Ministry*, World Council of Churches' Faith and Order Paper No. 111, 1982, pp.25f
3. *A History of the Methodist Church in Great Britain, Volume 1*, 1965, p.242
4. Ibid, p.243
5. *The Constitutional Practice and Discipline of the Methodist Church, Volume 2*, (cited hereafter as '*CPD*'), 1999 edition, Standing Order 211(2)
6. Ibid., Standing Order 211(3)
7. Ibid., Standing Order 603
8. The Methodist Conference *Agenda*, 1999, p.210
9. *CPD*, Standing Order 500
10. Ibid., Standing Order 515(1)
11. Ibid., Standing Order 400A
12. Ibid.
13. The Methodist Conference *Agenda*, 1999, p.207
14. *CPD*, Standing Order 230
15. See *CPD*, Standing Order 561
16. *CPD*, Standing Order 424(3)
17. Ibid.
18. *CPD*, Standing Order 425(2)
19. *CPD*, Standing Order 425(3)

20. The text of the report, together with the comments of the President's Council and of the Faith and Order Committee, can be found in *Statements of the Methodist Church on Faith and Order, 1933-1983*, pp. 204-231
21. *The Book of Discipline of the United Methodist Church*, #514
22. Ibid., #527(1)
23. Ibid., #527(2)
24. Ibid., #520 – #522
25. Ibid, #401
26. *The Basic Doctrines and Statutes of the Iglesia Evangelica Metodista Portuguesa*, Article 16
27. *Sharing in the Apostolic Communion*, pp.30f
28. Canon C18
29. *Conversations between the Church of England and the Methodist Church: An Interim Statement*, 1958, p.25
30. For example in *Commitment to Mission and Unity*, 1996, p.12
31. Quoted in the Methodist Conference *Agenda*, 1998, p.99
32. *Called to Witness and Service – The Reuilly Common Statement*, 1999, p.30
33. *The Documents of Vatican II*, 1965, p.41
34. Ibid.
35. Ibid., p.44
36. Ibid., p.52
37. Ibid., p.43
38. Ibid.
39. See *Anglican-Moravian Conversations*, 1996, pp.89f
40. *Sacraments, Ministry, Ordination, Leuenberg Texts 2,* Lembeck, Germany, 1995, p.98
41. Ibid.
42. *The Meissen Agreement Texts*, Council for Christian Unity Occasional Paper 2, 1992, p.18
43. *Called to Witness and Service – The Reuilly Common Statement*, 1999, pp.31f
44. *Called to Common Mission*, #16
45. Ibid., #7
46. Ibid., #13
47. Ibid., #18
48. The Methodist Conference *Agenda*, 1985, p.571
49. *Statements of the Methodist Church on Faith and Order, 1933-1983*, p.215
50. *Commitment to Mission and Unity*, p.10

Holy Communion –
A Methodist Perspective

1. The Faith and Order Committee is aware that there is no existing overall Methodist statement on the important issue of eucharistic theology and practice, and has therefore begun to prepare a report for eventual presentation to the Conference. It is envisaged that this process will take a further two (or possibly three) years, and will include wide consultation and the gathering of evidence.

2. At the same time, the Committee is aware that eucharistic theology and practice features in the ecumenical conversations already under way in each part of Britain, and it will maintain close contact with those involved in the various conversations, so as to ensure a consistency of approach.

3. There have been numerous Conference reports on some aspects of this issue. These have mostly dealt with particular questions, notably 'who may preside?' and the participation of children. However, many other questions have not received the same attention. The Committee is also aware that there is a wide variety of practice in our churches. Practice and theology influence each other. Over the past three or four decades, many new influences (notably through the ecumenical movement) have come to bear upon our attitude to the Lord's Supper. Many of these are reflected in *The Methodist Worship Book*.

4. Many Methodists, themselves holding the Lord's Supper in high esteem, find it difficult to understand the differing emphases and practices of other, equally sincere Methodists. The very choice of name, 'Lord's Supper', 'Holy Communion' or 'Eucharist' itself reflects a variety of understandings and emphases. Sometimes our beliefs are not fully articulated until a change in practice is proposed, for example the introduction of a 'common cup', or a change in the arrangements for the distribution of the elements.

5. The Committee's aim is to produce a report which will be genuinely 'owned' by the Church as a whole, and also offer fruitful material both for reflection within our Church and for those others who seek to discover what Methodist belief and practice is.

6. The Committee will, of course, draw upon the vast body of material to be found in existing Conference reports and statements, in our hymnody and in authorized liturgies. It will also consider the substantial contributions that Methodist theologians have made to the literature on the subject. The Methodist Church has published, through various channels, a wide variety of educational, devotional and theological material relating to Holy Communion, and this will also be examined.

7. The Committee will welcome input from all parts of the Connexion. Some material will be gathered by a survey. Members of the Conference are invited to assist with this, and questionnaires will be distributed to them during the Conference. Anyone else who would like to take part in

this survey is invited to contact the convenor of the working party, the Revd Jonathan Kerry.

8 Contributions are also particularly invited on the following topics:

- Descriptions of the actual practice of particular churches, and reflections upon the reasons for them, and the significance of them. Which liturgies and hymns, and what kind of vessels, bread and wine are used? What happens to the remaining bread and wine after communion? What are the practical arrangements (seating/ standing/kneeling, movement, arrangement of furnishings, role of stewards, assistance with the distribution, etc.)?

- The frequency of celebration of the Lord's Supper now and in the past.

- Views upon the significance of the Lord's Supper - how important is it as a part of our common life, and what do we believe we are doing or is happening?

- Have people's views changed over the years and if so, how?

- What are our views on 'the open table', and our participation in communion services of other Christian traditions? How do we recognize with sensitivity the good conscience of those who do not feel able to participate?

- What is the ministry of communion stewards, and how might this be developed?

- How can those who preside, and all who participate be better prepared for celebrating the Lord's Supper?

- What changes have you seen in recent years, and how do you react to them?

- What future developments would you like to see in our practice?

RESOLUTIONS

7/10. The Conference receives the report and invites responses to be sent to the Secretary of the Faith and Order Committee, Dr Clive Marsh, by 30th June 2001.

7/11. The Conference directs the Faith and Order Committee to present a further report to the Conference of 2002 or 2003.

The Church and Sex Offenders

PREFACE

This report on *The Church and Sex Offenders* was adopted by the Methodist Conference in June 2000, along with a series of resolutions concerning the report's implementation and further work to be done (Section 9).

Section 7b of the Report is particularly important. The Conference resolved that the procedures set out there should be 'the practice of the Methodist Church when a person who has been convicted of or has received a formal caution in respect of a sexual offence seeks to become part of a local church community'. Ministers and churches seeking further help and advice in developing and implementing this practice can obtain it from the Methodist Church's Regional Training and Development Officers or from Methodist Church House.

The Report covers very important issues both within the Church and society. We hope that church groups will study it, whether or not there is a convicted or cautioned sex offender in their community. The issues are of importance to all churches and concern the kind of community we seek to be. (Resolution 2(a) describes this as 'a community of love, forgiveness and reconciliation' committed to 'the restoration of broken people and communities'.)

To the end of the Report adopted by Conference we have added Appendices D and E. Appendix D offers Biblical material and a litany for groups studying the report. Appendix E contains a short list of recommended resources.

THE REPORT OF A WORKING PARTY
SET UP BY THE METHODIST COUNCIL

CONTENTS

1   INTRODUCTION AND EXECUTIVE SUMMARY

This report has been produced in response to a Notice of Motion to the 1997 Methodist Conference calling for a group to be set up *'to consider the ways in which appropriate and informed pastoral support and care may be given to those in the local church and community who have committed sexual offences.'* The particular context for the bringing of the Notice of Motion and for the work of the working party was the development of the Methodist Church's Safeguarding procedures (relating to good practice in work with children and young people) and, in particular, the decision of Conference not to allow people with convictions or police cautions for sex offences to hold office in the Church. Concern was expressed that, while it was clearly the Church's responsibility to do everything possible to protect children and young people from abuse, there was a danger that sex offenders would find no place in the life of the Church and that the gospel and ministry of the Church would thus be limited.

The working party wishes to state clearly at the outset of this report that it became increasingly aware, during the course of its work, of the wider implications of any statement, decision or change of practice relating to child protection issues. Something done to protect children or survivors may appear to exclude offenders. A piece of work aimed at including offenders may put children at risk or cause great pain or offence to those who have experienced sexual violence or abuse and who live with continuing physical, emotional and spiritual pain. The 1997 Report to Conference on Sexual Harassment and Abuse alerted the Church to this experience of survivors and victims and led to the development of new complaints and discipline procedures. The Safeguarding procedures have sought to improve our practice, particularly in work with children and young people, and have made us more aware of child protection issues within the life and activities of churches. This current report addresses issues relating to the place of sex offenders within the church community and beyond. The working party believes that far too little has been done to address the experience and needs of victims and survivors. Serious attention should now be paid to this issue by the Methodist Church, preferably in collaboration with other Churches. (See Resolution 38/4(a).)

The working party has received evidence from a wide variety of sources (see section 2) and tried to bring together insights from different disciplines. We have attempted in this report to set out what is known about sex offenders and have concluded that, while therapeutic interventions during and after custodial sentences may have some effect on future behaviour and reduce the risk of future offending, it is more appropriate to talk of sex offenders as 'recovering' than 'recovered' or 'cured'. Even if they participate in a therapeutic programme whilst in prison (and many offenders do not), when they have served their sentence they need continuing support from other people to help them rebuild and conduct their lives in a way which manages the thoughts, feelings, behaviours and situations which, in the past, have moved them towards offending.

For Christians, there are theological questions to be considered, particularly about how we understand conversion, restitution, forgiveness and a call to service. Can God change people's lives? Is God's forgiveness truly for all (or at least all who repent)? If we answer these questions in the affirmative, how can that be squared with the Methodist Church's Safeguarding procedures which appear to offer no way back into church office for someone who has been convicted or given a police caution for sexual offences against children? The working party looked at these questions in depth and saw that, whilst God can and does change people's lives and can and does offer forgiveness to all, there is and can be no sure and objective test by which we know when that has happened. The individual's testimony may be true, or it may not. Good intentions expressed at a time of heightened religious experience do not always work out in practice (something which is true for all of us). Some sex offenders who have testified to their conversion and to God's ongoing work in their lives have then re-offended. Given the nature of sex offending, an offender's acceptance of God's forgiveness is most likely to be reflected in an ongoing response in penitence, with the offender accepting a firm code of conduct for his new life in the congregation and in Christ.

The report considers some of the pastoral implications of the presence of sex offenders in congregations. It makes recommendations on appropriate practice both to safeguard children and young people and to enable sex offenders to take their place within the worship and fellowship of the Church. Given the tendency on the part of the media to demonise paedophiles and make it very difficult for sex offenders to rebuild their lives after the completion of their sentence, we believe the Church has a significant role to play in offering them and their families pastoral support and working alongside other agencies to encourage their responsible involvement in church and society.

While women can and sometimes do commit sex offences (and sometimes play a role in assisting a male perpetrator, perhaps by 'grooming' children), less than 5% of sex offences are known to involve female perpetrators. As the vast majority of perpetrators are male, we have described the offender as 'he' throughout this report.

2   HOW THE WORKING PARTY DID ITS WORK

a. Meetings

The working party held ten meetings at which it decided its work plan, received papers and documents prepared by members and others, heard evidence and discussed the principles involved. A draft of the report was circulated to many of those who had been consulted during the process for comment and discussed by the Pastoral Care and Christian Education Committee. The working party is very grateful to all those who submitted evidence and contributed to the process, including:

   i. Donald Findlater, describing the therapeutic approach and experience of the Faithfull Foundation's Wolvercote Clinic in its work with sex offenders;

  ii. The Revd Peter Sedgewick, of the General Synod Board for Social Responsibility, regarding the Church of England's work leading to the publication *Meeting the challenge: how churches should respond to sex offenders*;

 iii. Nicolas Coote, the Secretary of the Catholic Bishops' Conference, describing similar work being done in the Roman Catholic Church;

 iv. Offenders who wrote to us of their experience and hopes upon release;

  v. Survivors - we were able to draw on the pastoral and personal experience of members of the working party and on work done in preparing the 1997 Conference Report on Sexual Harassment and Abuse. In the Autumn of 1999, Churches Together in Britain and Ireland published Margaret Kennedy's *The Courage to Tell*, which added to our understanding of survivors' experience of 'church' and faith (and which we feel is important, if painful, reading for the Church as a whole);

 vi. Detective Inspector Tim Bryan of the Metropolitan Police, who outlined the relevant legislation relating to sex offenders, particularly the recent Acts regarding registration;

 vii. Jan Davies and Michael Roberts, of Middlesex Probation Service, who described procedures relating to sex offenders in the community and the work of Risk Management Panels;

viii. Andrew Cordy, who described the role of Prison chaplains and provided insight into the therapeutic programmes run for sex offenders in prison;

 ix. several Circuit ministers who described their experience in churches and circuits where sex offenders had become involved;

  x. Chris Wood and James West, who outlined the work of Katherine Price Hughes House, West London Mission's Probation Hostel.

b. Reporting date

It soon became apparent that to produce the report would take longer than the time originally allowed, so the working party asked the Methodist Council for permission to delay bringing its report until Conference in 2000. This permission was granted.

c. A survey of ministers

In order to ascertain whether the rehabilitation of sex offenders was a significant issue within the Church, in February 1999 the working party circulated a questionnaire to the ministers of five synods (see Appendix B). Ministers were asked about their experience of working with offenders and victims/survivors in their current appointment and throughout the whole of their ministry.

13.3% of ministers said they knew of offenders in their current appointment, though the percentage varied from 25% in North Wales to 4.2% in South Wales (with Chester & Stoke 10.9%, London North West 20% and Cymru 5.3%). It is interesting to note the differences between Districts, which may reflect the experience in some Districts of providing ongoing pastoral support for those involved in particular cases (e.g. of historic abuse in residential care homes). Overall, about one fifth (19.6%) of ministers (ranging from 41.7% in North Wales to 8.3% in South Wales) said that they had known of sexual offenders becoming involved in the church at some point during their ministry. While these figures indicate that a significant proportion of ministers are aware of sex offenders in the life of the Church, evidence from the Faithfull Foundation suggests the actual number to be higher than these findings indicate. It seems likely that ministers are frequently unaware of sex offenders who are present in churches.

Ministers were more aware of offenders returning to their previous church and community than of them arriving at a church at which they were previously unknown. Of course, ministers and the community are more likely to know about a sex offender who returns to his previous home after release. A sex offender moving to a new area may not announce his arrival.

One minister who responded to the questionnaire had developed a ministry to adult survivors of abuse and had a large number of such survivors in the congregation. The working party warmly welcomed such a vital ministry and would like to encourage more work in this area.

3   WHAT WE KNOW ABOUT SEX OFFENDING

a. What is a sexual offence?

A working definition is an offence in which a person seeks to gain emotional and/or physical gratification from inappropriate and illegal sexual contact and activities with another person against their will and/or who is below the age of legal consent. Some offenders engage in very specific acts with very specific individuals or types of individual as their target (adult or child, male or female); for others the range of acts and victims will be much wider and less specific. Our report is about sex offenders in general, though the Church's Safeguarding procedures relate specifically to those convicted of or cautioned for offences against children and the Church has a particular responsibility to protect children and young people from abuse.

The types of sexual offences are set out in Appendix C. These, however, are for the most part broad categories and embrace a very wide range of acts on the part of an offender. It may be more helpful, therefore, to give some examples from specific categories. An indecent assault on a male could range from touching of genitalia over or under clothing, oral sex on the victim, masturbating them, kissing, fondling of any part of the body or digital penetration. An act of gross indecency with a child may involve an offender in exposing himself, getting the child to pose for him, taking indecent photographs, getting a child to masturbate him or masturbating himself in front of a child. Serious criminal offences against a female may include oral, anal or vaginal penetration.

The emotional pleasure and satisfaction gained by the offender may be related not only to sexual gratification, but also to a sense of control and power exercised over his victim.

b. Who are sex offenders?

It is difficult to estimate the number of sex offenders. Some have been convicted or cautioned. Many have not. A Home Office study in 1995 showed that if the Sex Offenders Register had been in effect since 1953, 125,000 offenders would have to register, 25,000 of these for life. Most incidents of child sexual abuse are not reported (current estimates suggest 5-8 % are reported to a statutory agency) and currently in the UK only a minority of reported cases result in prosecution,. A smaller proportion leads to a conviction, so those actually convicted of sexual offences are a very small proportion of those likely to have offended.

Offenders come from every social group and category, irrespective of profession, level of intelligence, educational background, ability, sexual orientation, nationality, religion or age. Most, but not all, sex offenders are male (less than 5% of sex offences are known to involve female perpetrators). Approximately one third are adolescents. Many sexual offenders committed their first offence as adolescents, but by no means all adolescent offenders go on to become adult offenders. While media coverage often stereotypes sex offenders as less than human, outsiders with no connections to families or communities, this does not reflect what is currently known about them. The majority of offences against children are committed by individuals known to the child and often by the family. 80% of offences against children are committed in their home or in that of the perpetrator. Girls are more likely to be abused within the family, boys outside. Histories of individual offending can range between a single event within or outside the family to ongoing abuse over years. A USA study based on the 'self reports' of 411 convicted sex offenders, given immunity from prosecution in regard to past offences, showed that they had an average of 533 offences and 336 victims each. Offenders did not limit themselves to one type of offence. Many had abused boys and girls, adults and children, and children within and outside their families.

The charges for which individuals are convicted are often "specimen" charges, the ones where there is the strongest evidence and/or where a guilty plea can be gained in return for dropping more serious charges. This has the effect of the reducing the penalty.

Some offenders are socially isolated, with poor social skills and low self esteem. Others may be articulate, well educated and hold responsible positions. They are all extremely skilled in techniques to target and entrap children, and in establishing positions of trust and authority which afford ready access to children. There is also no direct link between being abused and becoming an offender, though many offenders speak of trauma experienced in their own childhood. The reality is that offenders are people whom we know and in some cases like, and who can and will manipulate individuals and organizations, including churches, to gain access to children.

There is no higher rate of mental illness recorded amongst those who commit sexual offences than amongst the general population. In other words, there is no standard psychopathology of sexual offending to which it can be attributed. Sexual offending is not an illness, it is a behaviour consciously undertaken with the knowledge that it is regarded by the majority of people as being morally repugnant and that the discovery will involve relatively severe punitive sanctions, social ostracism and outrage.

c. Why do people commit sexual offences?

Explanations range across the historical, sociological, cultural, psychological and biological. Some arise from empirical research, others out of clinical observations, and others out of vested interest. Consequently, they are built on radically different foundations and to present even a limited review of the theories and literature available would require much space. What is set out here is an integrated theory which is the most widely acknowledged explanation of sexual offending and which is complex and tentative. (N.B. There are different theories, but not as yet much information, regarding female offenders.)

The theory argues that because of their genetic make up, males have a greater tendency towards aggressive behaviour than do women. This may be overcome, in the majority of males, through learning appropriate and acceptable ways of relating to and behaving towards women as they grow and develop in families and society. The vast majority of males have no desire to, and do not, commit sexual offences. If, however, appropriate behaviour is not established – for example because of poor parental example or lack of affection – then sex and aggression may become fused. Social and cultural attitudes may also exercise an important influence. As a society we need to be made more aware of the standards and messages we adopt and convey which may, advertently or inadvertently, suggest that women are to be seen as objects of sexual pleasure for others; that men 'can't help themselves'; that children are precocious; etc. Such messages feed into the 'permission giving' discussed below and encourage a negative view of women and their role. (The 1997 Report on Sexual Harassment and Abuse described a number of situations in which behaviour reflecting this kind of view was experienced within the Church.) This, along with a failure to develop appropriate social skills and sexual experience can enhance the likelihood of moving towards offending. The availability and use of pornography may reinforce already negative attitudes as well as heighten the desire for sexual gratification. Drugs and alcohol may also be used to dis-inhibit by a person who may otherwise feel moral constraints or fear for the consequences. Add a context in which he feels he will not be caught and the likelihood of offending is even more increased.

This model allows for a variety of factors to converge without presupposing that any single one must pertain or dominate. It gives perspective, therefore, to the wide range of experiences and attitudes, which may be encountered in offenders, all of which may be relevant in their choosing to offend.

d. How do sex offenders perpetrate their crime?

There is a series of steps an offender will follow leading up to the execution of his crime. This model remains true for all offenders, including non-sexual, but it is particularly helpful in understanding how sex offenders operate. The order is always sequential but the time scale for each step as well as the whole may vary from just a few minutes to many years. For example, an offender began to fantasize about sexual acts with a child in his late teens/early twenties but it was not until almost forty years later that he committed his first offence. Another offender began to fantasize about touching a woman's breasts in a busy town centre; within half an hour he had committed an offence.

i. *Wanting to offend*

In the case of the sex offender this will be a desire to fulfil an emotional or physical need through some form of illegal sexual activity. Some offenders will have a very clear mental image of what it is they want to do and the type of (or actual) person to whom they want to do it. For others it will be much more vague. For some there will be in place well-rehearsed and developed fantasies which they are seeking the opportunity to enact and to which a victim's face may be added. For others the fantasy will be much more mundane and non-specific. There is not necessarily a direct cause and effect relationship between what is in the mind of the offender and the actual offence.

ii. *Giving himself permission*

Most sex offenders know that what they want to do is wrong. In order to proceed, therefore, they have to put in place a way of thinking which overcomes their inhibitions and give themselves permission to carry out the desired act. This way of thinking has to deal with past as well as potential offences and will ultimately lead some offenders to the belief that what they are doing is all right and not harmful to their victims. This may be further developed by the belief that it is not their own, but society's perception of what they do, which is mistaken.

This distorted cognitive process falls into three main categories.

(a) Making reprehensible conduct socially and ethically acceptable. There may be moral justifications ('it's sex education'; 'it will be better for her to learn from me than from a stranger'; 'she's my step daughter not my natural daughter'; 'it was a proper relationship'; 'I was showing him the affection he didn't get at home'); psychological justification ('it happened because my wife and I weren't getting on'; 'I was drunk at the time'; 'it's because of my own abuse - I can't help it'); palliative comparisons ('I only touched her, I didn't penetrate her'; 'at least it's not a boy'; 'it won't hurt her'); or euphemistic labelling ('I was only fooling around - it just happened' and 'we were only playing').

(b) Misconstruing the consequences of the behaviour. This may involve minimizing the consequences ('the child didn't suffer'; 'I won't do any harm'; 'he didn't say anything so he must have been enjoying it'; 'I only intend it to be a bit of fun'); misattribution of the consequences ('it's the way that other people perceive it or deal with it that causes the problems for the child'); or ignoring the consequences ('I don't care').

(c) Devaluing or attributing blame to the victim, either by dehumanisation of the victim ('she was a slag') or by attribution of blame ('she was asking for it the way she was dressed'; 'you know what children are like from an early age these days - she came on to me').

For many offenders this distorted thinking will be accompanied by denial, which covers a wide spectrum but will often have some very specific aspects. There may be: denial of intention ('I did touch her but it was an accident and it certainly wasn't sexual'); denial of the event ('it never happened, she just wanted to get her own back on me'); denial which is supported by family and friends ('they know what he's like and they are supporting me'); psychological denial ('do I seem to you like the kind of person who could do such a thing?'); the denial of need for any kind of therapeutic intervention in their abusive behaviour ('when I was in prison I found God and became a Christian and now I see things clearly'; 'Jesus has healed me - I no longer have any 'bad' thoughts'). This latter form of denial, where a claim of religious experience or conversion is used as a reason not to need therapy, is particularly relevant in the context of this report.

Through such distorted thinking and the associated denial an offender overcomes his sense of culpability and guilt about past and potential offences and the impact on his victims.

iii. Creating the opportunity to offend

In essence the focus here is on getting into a position which gives access to a particular (or range of) potential victim(s).

It may be something as simple as walking home by a particular route so that contact is made with a child or children at a specific location. It could be deliberately engaging in activities, for example scouting, which provide the opportunity to be a significant person in charge of a group of potential victims. It could be achieved by entering a specific profession, for example teaching or Christian ministry. It could be that an offender might take a job with working hours which allow or necessitate being alone with his children. It could be going to a place, for example a pub or club, where there are likely to be a lot of lone females. Often it involves making friends with the parents of a child. Babysitting of nephews, nieces and grandchildren may be 'generously' offered by offenders. Encouragement of a partner to go out with friends or take up some activity in the evening, leaving you alone with the children is a seemingly 'caring' and 'supportive' act. Generous attention and friendship given to the vulnerable and under-privileged may attract admiration from others.

Sexual offenders are often described as 'grooming' individuals, families and communities. This can take many months or even years, during which the offender builds a relationship and develops opportunities. Rarely does the individual creating the opportunity to offend draw attention to himself through other forms of anti-social behaviour. On the contrary, offenders present themselves in a whole variety of acceptable ways - the self-assured professional, the 'nice old gentleman' who lives down the street, the 'not very bright' but 'harmless' man, the happy family man, the man who's had a 'hard time' and needs some help and support.

iv.   Overcoming the victim's resistance

Physical strength and size, violence and the threat of violence, are certainly factors in overcoming the victim's resistance to sexual assault. In many cases, however, it is much more subtle.

Offending is rarely against complete strangers and considerable thought, time, patience and effort may go into establishing a compliant victim. For example, a 'date rape' victim has usually had some previous, if limited, physical contact with the perpetrator; a child may be groomed from a very early age to accept touching and eventually penetration as 'normal'; isolation of a child within a family setting may make them feel that the consequences of speaking out could mean exclusion from what gives them security; in other cases of familial abuse a child may have the thought implanted that they will be responsible for the break-up of the family unit if they were to report their abuse; the significance and standing of an abuser to the victim may imply that no one would believe them should they disclose; vulnerable victims may be susceptible to 'rewards' for their 'co-operation'; emotional as well as physical conditioning by the offender may create a 'willingness' for the victim to participate for fear of losing the 'relationship' or 'friendship'; the inference of a 'reputation' and the imparting of a sense of culpability and guilt may deter adults from reporting sexual attacks. Ever present is the idea of secrecy, personal responsibility and unpleasant consequences for the victim who discloses.

e. Sentences for sexual offences

Most convicted sex offenders receive custodial sentences. A few are given Probation Orders or other community penalties. A Probation Order normally requires an offender to be part of a programme (such as those offered at the West London Mission's Katherine Price Hughes House) to address their sexual offending.

f. Towards a new life

The brief overview given above demonstrates that the issue of the pastoral care and support of sex offenders must be approached with a good deal of understanding and the absence of sentimentality. Even if they participate in them, sex offenders are not 'cured' by therapeutic programmes and will continue to have a predisposition towards offending. The 1995 Home Office study quoted earlier showed that within five years of their first conviction, 10% of sexual offenders had another conviction for a sexual offence and 22% for either a sexual or a violent offence.

Evidence suggests that completion of treatment can reduce, but by no means remove, the likelihood of further convictions. The Working Party received evidence from Donald Findlater of the Faithfull Foundation; the The Revd Andrew Cordy, a full-time prison chaplain who is a Facilitator in the Offending Behaviour Programme Unit; and Chris Wood and James West of the West London Mission. Those programmes that have been seen as most successful both look at behaviour and develop strategies for the offender to avoid situations where they are likely to offend. The year's programme with the Faithfull Foundation can also include work with the offender's family and support networks (including the local church) to show what risk he presents and help them to help him manage his behaviour so as to avoid risk situations in the future.

Several of those who gave evidence to the working party suggested that sex offending could be seen as an addiction, in some ways like alcoholism. (While there are similarities between sex offending and alcoholism and other addictions, there is a major difference in so far as the main victim of sex offending is, of course, not the offender.) An offender cannot claim to be 'recovered' but might be described as 'recovering'. As with the Alcoholics Anonymous' twelve steps programme, a person needs ongoing awareness and ongoing support. It is important that the offender's memory of what he did continues.

The following is a summary of the factors that are currently believed to reduce the risk of re-offending. These factors merely indicate a reduced likelihood of re-offending. No single factor in itself indicates reduced risk.

* First time conviction.
* Realizing the enormity of what they have done, admitting their responsibility and the harm their sexual violence has caused.
* Completion of treatment.
* Support from family and friends on release.
* Establishment of a social network.
* Avoidance of situations involving contact with children.
* Participation in ongoing treatment and agreement to monitoring.

A report by the Inspectorate of Probation [HMIP 1998] stated that at the end of 1996, 9000 sex offenders were on Probation Service case loads, 4338 were in custody and 4763 were in the community. In regard to those in the community, decisions have to be made about the possible risks that these offenders may pose. Simplistic models are not always helpful, as is illustrated by a number of cases where people convicted many years ago of offences deemed to be 'minor' have subsequently reoffended and been convicted of much more serious offences.

g. Preventing further offending – recent legislation

The 1990s saw the introduction of several pieces of legislation relating to sex offenders.

The Criminal Justice Act 1991
On release from prison, sex offenders sentenced under this Act are subject to statutory supervision by police, probation and other professionals. Offenders sentenced before 1991 were not subject to such monitoring and the whereabouts of many of them are unknown, though legislation in 1998 allows Orders to be made regarding those sex offenders seen as most potentially dangerous.

The Sex Offenders Act 1997
This introduced the registration of sex offenders released from 1st September 1997, but was not retrospective. Under this Act, offenders are required to register with the local police within fourteen days of become resident in a new area. The sanction for not registering is a three to six month prison sentence. The requirement continues for periods of five, seven or ten years or for life if the custodial sentence was for thirty months or more. (For juveniles the period is half.) When an offender registers, police then work with other appropriate agencies to establish the level of risk and the level of dangerousness or harm posed by the offender. In each area a monthly risk management meeting shares information about known offenders and looks at case management plans around known risks. Risk management panels are generally chaired by police or probation, but include representatives from other appropriate agencies. (These procedures are still relatively new and there may be inconsistencies in how they operate in different areas.) It was suggested to the working party that the church should expect to be involved in this process in appropriate cases, but this will depend on the development of necessary skills, understanding and credibility on the church's part. Where an offender joins a church, the offender's probation officer may well be willing to discuss the risk factors with the church, along with ways of managing the offender's behaviour. If the officer does not approach the church, the church should approach the officer.

The Crime and Disorder Act 1998.
This made it possible to make a Sex Offender Order and to register Schedule 1 offenders sentenced before 1997 and seen to be a continuing threat.

h. Providing support

What is known about offenders, and the way in which they gain access to children, has to lead us to be extremely cautious in regard to their contact with children, young people and vulnerable adults. We also have to bear in mind that most offenders are not reported or prosecuted. Given this, communities need to be aware that offenders target vulnerable children and young people, and gain the trust and respect of caring adults. Grooming of the adults is a crucial part of the targeting of children, when offenders can assess the support systems available to children and how effective they are. Clear messages must be given that children, young people and adult survivors are listened to, believed and their stories acted upon. Offenders and potential offenders need to know that abuse of children, young people or anyone else is wholly wrong and unacceptable.

A critical factor in the likelihood of re-offending is the level of informed and consistent support offenders receive when they return to the community. The truth is that, outside of the statutory authorities (and that only whilst they are on a licence), the majority have little or no support from family or friends and no public sympathy because of the nature of their crimes. More adult support could and should be offered to known offenders in our communities. However, those offering support should be aware of the person's offences and be able to challenge behaviour that would put the offender in a situation where they are likely to re-offend.

The working party believes that the Church can play a significant role in developing these all important circles of support which will not only provide care for the individual offender but also help to reduce the number of future victims from abuse and contribute directly to public well-being. It is important that the Church takes this role seriously, as it is clear that many sex offenders see church attendance as part of their life both during and after their prison sentence. In his evidence to the Working Party, Donald Findlater said that almost 25% of sex offenders involved in programmes at the Wolvercote Clinic and other centres he had contacted attend church weekly (compared to 8-9% of the general population). Why there is such a link between sex offending and church attendance is not totally clear and raises interesting questions, not least that of how far the church is part of the problem and/or the solution.

4   SOME THEOLOGICAL QUESTIONS

The issues surrounding the experience of sex offending and the restoration into the church's life of those who offend raise many fundamental theological matters. We confine ourselves to the three most commonly raised during our work and in the general discussions in the Church press.

a. Forgiveness

Every Christian knows that the strong statement "Your sins are forgiven" is central to the gospel news. It reverberates through the Bible and our liturgies, is sought whenever we say the Lord's Prayer, is sung about with great joy and lies deep within Christian awareness. Whatever you have done and been in the past, God offers forgiveness.

> *And every offender who truly believes,*
> *That moment from Jesus a pardon receives:*
> (Hymns and Psalms 463)

However, there are many differences within the Church as to what such forgiveness means and entails. There are many Protestants, especially those within the holiness traditions, who believe that to be forgiven by God means that the past is eradicated so that a forgiven sinner is henceforth treated as if those sins never were. They are "blotted out". The forgiven sinner starts life again in such a fresh way as to be morally clean. The wonder of justification is precisely this - to be pronounced innocent in Christ.

Many Christians do not interpret the New Testament teaching and our experience in this way. It tends to be simplistic concerning the ongoing mystery of sin, to neglect the social character of our sinning (which is against our neighbour as well as against God) and to be romantic about actual Christian discipleship and its struggles. Thus there are three common misunderstandings we should avoid:

i. Forgiveness means 'forgetting'. The injured one says to the offender, "I forget what you did". If God does this then God is promoting an unreal world in which history has to be constantly rewritten and in which offended persons are expected to ignore traumas and injuries they have suffered. But the great story of the Old Testament is not like this: Israel's sins are constantly rehearsed for all to remember.

ii. Forgiveness means the cancelling of debts and obligations. Instead it may well mean the offender having a greater sense of obligation than before (as with Zaccheus who, after encountering Christ, offered to repay four times those he had swindled, even though the law only required it to be twofold). Thus forgiveness should encourage the offender to take responsibility for the damage caused and for seeking to rectify the situation or make restitution (e.g by paying for the survivor's therapy?) US pastoral theologian, Marie Fortune, tells of a group of incest offenders in a treatment programme whose powerful plea was, 'Don't forgive so easily.' All were Christians and all had asked their pastors for forgiveness. Prayers had been said. They'd been forgiven and sent home. All the offenders said this pastoral response was not helpful because it enabled them to avoid accountability for what they had done.

iii. Forgiveness means being treated as wholly reformed and good. Quite often offenders argue that they have become totally new people and therefore don't need therapeutic intervention. To see forgiveness in this way would be naïve. Forgiveness helps us on the road to Christian maturity, but does not suddenly place us at the end of our pilgrimage. A sober reading of Romans 7 reminds us that like Paul "I do not do the good I want", and that is still our condition. Being forgiven by God and neighbour does not lift us out of that perpetual perversity which is our human nature.

To be positive, in forgiveness God is saying, "I accept you totally. Despite what you did and were, you are reconciled. In the wonder of Christ I am with you to rebuild your life and put the past right. By the energy of the Holy Spirit live now as a new person, be forgiving too and be full of hope." When we forgive each other we are offering the human level of such goodness.

But it does not stop there. The New Testament makes it clear that God is also constantly saying, "Have the mind that was in Christ. Keep on walking by the Spirit. Cultivate new graces and new wisdom." In the Lord's Prayer we ask forgiveness from God, but that is immediately followed by the request not to be led into temptation or put "to the test". In the context of our concerns that is especially important; the forgiven one must be learning more of his or her self and how to avoid the special weaknesses each of us is prone to. We are called to a radically new life, significantly different from the old, and we have to take responsibility for ensuring that life will be different and that we avoid situations which put ourselves and others at risk. This implies a personal discipline that builds up those inner restraints and desires that help us on to maturity in Christ.

Now we face two ongoing problems. Is forgiveness dependent upon the offender being penitent? Must the sinner experience the full scope of what the New Testament called 'metanoia', a total turning away from evil so as to face in a new direction? There is much clear teaching to this effect. "If another disciple sins, you must rebuke the offender, and if there is repentance, you must forgive." (Luke 17.3.) "If we confess our sins, he who is faithful and just will forgive us our sins." (1 John 1.9.) Yet there are many instances where Jesus apparently forgave sinners and later said "Sin no more" and there is no hint of their contrition (e.g. the woman caught in adultery in John 7.53 - 8.11). The dying criminal on the cross beside Jesus is forgiven, it seems (Luke 23.43). The father runs to meet the returning prodigal son long before a word can be spoken.

This could well mean that we should be forgiving even when the response of penitence has not yet been expressed. Maybe the discovery that one has been forgiven promotes penitence and the fitting response? Maybe we are to understand God's forgiveness as being prevenient? A scholar wrote to say, "I suspect that the tension we find here cannot be eradicated."

The second problem is that of the sin which cannot be forgiven, as in Mark 3.28f and parallels, and the sin which is 'mortal' (1 John 5.16). The context makes it clear that this is not a specific sort of sin against another person - say a sexual sin - but that sort of disposition which rejects God, scorns Christ and his ministry and maybe a conscience repudiating any sense of obligation to God or need for mercy from him.

We were greatly exercised by the question as to how readily victims of sexual offences and survivors of abuse should be expected to forgive their abusers. This forgiveness has sometimes been bluntly commanded within the Church, but to expect immediate forgiveness has been pastorally unwise, grievously insensitive and unrealistic. In the long run God calls us to forgive our enemies and his commands are for our good; in the short run it may be both impossible and undesirable, though it may eventually happen almost as a 'by-product' at the end of a long, hard process of recovery. It may be quite wrong for an abused person to meet the offender again, and always wrong for an offender to try to coerce a victim into forgiveness and reconciliation.

b. Conversion

At the heart of the gospel is the power of God to transform people's lives for good.

> *If anyone is in Christ, there is a new creation: everything old has passed away; see, everything has become new.* (2 Cor. 5.17)

The way into this new life may be by a sudden transforming event, or more frequently by a process lasting a few years. It does crucial things for us:-

- it gives us an overwhelming sense of the coming of God to us in Jesus Christ. God is for us, with us, in us, in Christ. Hallelujah!
- it introduces us to radically new aims, purposes, values, and the chance to live for and in the New One, Jesus Christ.
- it enables us to 'make the best' of the initial *persona* we are given. We are forgiven; make a new start.
- it invites us into the life of the Church, the nourishment of 'the means of grace' and the life of the Christian community.
- it calls us to witness to our faith, to have a ministry, to serve the world, to love God and neighbour.
- even though we become more acutely aware of our failures, sins, weaknesses, we are ushered into the world of God's promises and given constant hope.
- it requires and enables us to accept the discipline and direction of the Church.

There are many things that conversion does not do:-

- it does not change our origins, parentage, nationality, first language, age, gender.
- it does not change our physical structure, our height, weight, capacity to see or hear, facility at music or sports.
- it does not change our basic mental/emotional structure. Our IQ remains what it was before. Those especially sensitive to pain remain so; those who are dyslexic remain so.
- it does not stop us sinning. As before, we are tempted, often confused and baffled, and subject to the strange inner law which means that we do not do what we want to do.
- it does not insulate us from all the dangers, illnesses, tragedies and accidents that are the stuff of ordinary life.
- it does not cure sexual offending or the temptation to offend.

We do not lose heart. Even though our outer nature is wasting away, our inner nature is being renewed day by day. (2 Cor. 4.10)

c. Church discipline

It is clear from passages like Matthew 18, 1 Corinthians 6 or 10, or 1 Timothy, that the early Church practised a strong discipline for its members and leaders. It never assumed that conversion to Christ so transformed the believer's character as to render firm control and order unnecessary. On the contrary it enjoined this firmness on all and appeared to have little reluctance to expel uncooperative members who sinned flagrantly (as in 1 Corinthians 5.2 or Hebrews 6.4). The discipline was an integral part of the Church being an agency of the gospel, a school for forgiveness.

Suppose now that a sexual offender joins a church. How should that church respond? Not by a "quick fix" offering ready acceptance with few questions asked and little of the awful past acknowledged. That would be unworthy, unfair on the offender's previous victim(s), dangerous for the congregation's own 'little ones' and very bad indeed for the offender. That person now needs a new framework for life and what Wesley called 'the wisdom working from above', a wisdom involving no naivety, moral carelessness or illusions. Instead it should be offering strong hope through the practice of good discipline.

This would presume ongoing penitence by the offender, this being both the precondition and result of the forgiving experience, causing the person to say something like this - "I am so grateful that God and now the church have forgiven me that I gladly resolve to live differently. As a sex offender I acknowledge what I have done and the harm it caused others. So I accept limitations on where I go and whom I meet as signs of my genuine desire to lead a new life." Some in the Roman Catholic Church argue that priests who have sexually abused children should be told that "If you are truly penitent you must be prepared to offer a tangible sign (i.e. your ministry)." Penitence would also become evident through a proper, wholehearted engagement with ongoing treatment provision and working with the risk management panel and others who are part of the support network.

What would the discipline consist of? That would depend upon the particular individual. In most cases it would probably mean meeting with a small group of Christians regularly and 'in band'; regular worship and a nourishing spiritual lifestyle; an unequivocal pledge to keep clear of 'temptation situations'; a readiness to share deeply of oneself, one's past misuse of power over others, attempts to hide from reality and minimize one's sins; a constantly renewed desire to learn how to centre life on Christ and not on self, and thus learn the ways of love. (See further section 7b.)

Should this discipline be so immutable that the offender can never be involved in church leadership and its offices? No one has a 'right' to hold office in the Church. We may offer, but it is for the Church to confer the office. Authority is conferred and to be exercised as servant of The Servant - and servant ministry is incompatible with 'rights' language.

We accept the widespread conviction that sexual offenders are permanently a grave risk to others. It is, therefore, appropriate in their own interests, and in those of survivors, potential victims and the wider community, for them not to hold office in the Church. Living a safe Christian life is itself a calling from God. However, we also note the plain fact that in time God's grace can work healing wonders in the most damaged personality (which we term 'the optimism of grace'). Always the last word rests with God, with the promise of the new, with the coming of Christ. We found this issue to be especially difficult, but thought that the Church must have a way to respond in very exceptional circumstances (and return to this matter in Section 5.b).

5   CLARIFYING THE ISSUES

a. Child protection

All the members of the working party and all those who gave evidence to it stressed the importance of the Church doing all it can to safeguard children and young people in its care. This has implications in the recruitment, training and support of those who work with children and young people; it means continuing to develop good practice in our children's and youth work and in all our church life; it means developing sensitivity to children and young people we have contact with who may be being abused at home or elsewhere; and it means an increased awareness of the needs of adults who have been victims of sexual offences or who were sexually abused as children. Nobody suggested to the working party that these issues were not important or that the Church should accept low standards of care in matters of child protection.

b. Holding office within the church

We believe that sex offenders have a place within the Church. The issue is about how to balance the welfare of the sex offender with the needs of the wider church community, especially the welfare of children and survivors of abuse. As noted earlier, there is particular controversy around the question of whether a person who has been convicted of a sexual offence should, in effect, be banned for life from holding office in the Church. It is clear that a person who has committed violent or sexual offences against children should not be given responsibility for work with children and young people, but may be less clear why such a person should be barred from other jobs. Of course, some roles that are not directly given responsibility for children nonetheless might allow access to them. But there are other roles that don't allow lone access to premises or face-to-face contact with children and young people. Surely, some argue, these could be open to a convicted or cautioned sex offender? The working party believes not. To place an offender in such a position can (and frequently does) cause deep offence to survivors who are members of the congregation. What is more, by appointing someone to office with a high profile or representative capacity, a church is saying 'This is a trusted, respected person.' This invites parents and others to accept the person as trustworthy. Sexual offending is partly about misuse of power. Once in a position of trust and respect someone minded to do so can easily move from there into other positions of respect which give more opportunity of access to children. Churches attract vulnerable people and also provide ideal situations for the predatory and manipulative.

Against this it may be argued that to ban someone for life is to set limits on God's power to change people and therefore reflects a flawed and narrow doctrine of forgiveness. At the heart of the Christian gospel is the belief in the power of the Holy Spirit to transform people's lives and to offer them new beginnings. The Methodist Conference's Safeguarding procedures are seen by some to deny this 'good news'. Most of the members of the working party were firmly committed to the belief that God can and does transform people's lives. However, as we received evidence from those who work with sex offenders, it was clear that, while we do know quite a lot about rates of re-offending, there is not (and can never be) a sure test by which we know that a particular person has been transformed by God and will not re-offend. Indeed, it seemed that many sex offenders become involved in the life of the prison chapel and regularly attend worship during their sentence and many testify to a conversion experience, or to a renewal and deepening of faith. We were also confronted with the grim reality that some sexual offences are committed by converted, active church members. Avowed religious experience is no guarantee of safety from sexual offending. We were given from the Faithfull Foundation specific examples of church leaders who had offended, 'repented', been allowed to continue in Christian ministry and then offended again. Experience from the West London Mission's Katherine Price Hughes house suggested that many offenders said they had been converted.

Given all this, the working party does not believe that the current restriction should be lifted. However, as there is evident unease on the part of some within the Church who see the restriction as too inflexible, we believe consideration should be given to the possibility of suggesting that the Senior Persons Group (set up by the Methodist Council as part of the Safeguarding arrangements) be asked to consider (on the basis of risk assessment) any very exceptional case where it is believed a person should be able to take up office despite SO 010 (2) (ii). We make this recommendation (Resolution 38/5) very hesitatingly, as we found it difficult to identify situations where such a provision might be necessary. Two suggestions of possible exceptions made to the working party were:

(a) where the person is believed to have committed a very minor offence, a long time in the past, where there was no suggestion of lack of consent (e.g. where the act would have been seen as consensual were it not for the age of the girl being slightly under 16 and the boy being slightly over 16) and where the current risk is judged to be minimal, and

(b) where the law has changed since the offence was committed, and what was then an offence is no longer one.

We would recommend that the route to the Senior Persons' Group would be via the District Chairs.

c. Offences against adults

The working party became aware of what might be an anomaly in the Church's practice. We were asked to consider how *'appropriate and informed pastoral support and care may be given to those in the local church and community who have committed sexual offences.'* However, the issue was raised in response to the development of child protection procedures within the Church and the decision that people who had been convicted or received a police caution for sexual offences <u>against</u> <u>children</u> should not be able to hold office. So, what of those who have been convicted of sexual offences against adults? The working party believes consideration should be given to whether those who commit sexual offences against adults should be subject to the same or similar disciplines. Resolution 4c suggests this matter be referred to the Methodist Council.

6   PASTORAL PERSPECTIVES

This report has to deal with different perspectives which are inconsistent. This is true in many areas of church life, but perhaps particularly so in issues relating to sex offenders and the Church. We need to acknowledge the extent of pain and difficulty in pastoral situations that arise from incidents of sexual violence and abuse, whether it be the pain of survivors/victims, their families, the offenders and their families, the community, those responsible in that community, or the ministers and pastoral carers. From a pastoral point of view there is potentially a responsibility to all. Many believe that the pain of survivors needs to be paramount in our minds, but the main focus of this report (and the working party's brief) relates to offenders. We believe that providing appropriate support to offenders will also help prevent and minimize the risk of further offending. We therefore start this section of the report from the offender's perspective:

a. The offender's perspective

What does the sex offender need to receive from the church community as part of his rehabilitation? Acceptance, love, a place to worship and join in fellowship, comrades for the journey, and people who accept him as he is and commit themselves to supporting him in his attempt to live a new life as a recovering sex offender.

Offenders (not necessarily sex offenders) who wrote to the working party said:

My own personal concern is the validity of how people perceive my faith. Is it just a con? . . . But I can offer something . . . . To those who doubt, may I be an example, someone who people can see God working in.

I would like to think that I could be welcome in any community. I do not expect to be treated like a long lost son. I would like a chance to prove myself and not be "tarred with the same brush".

One offender told of his family's bad experience. His wife and nine-year-old daughter were initially welcomed in one church but 'at the mention of her husband being in prison she was shunned and made to feel most unwelcome.' This experience reminds us that it is not just the offender whose needs we have to consider. The offender's family will be living with all kinds of difficulties, in their own relationships (and with the offender) and in how they are perceived and treated by the wider community. There is a very significant role for churches here in offering care and support to families of offenders.

Another said he had had a similar experience:

In the past I have been made very unwelcome by churches outside prison. No sooner had I told them I was an ex-offender than they acted like I had told them I had leprosy.

Given this kind of response it may not be surprising when an offender prefers not to 'go public' about his past life.

Like anyone else, a sex offender has much both to contribute and receive within the Christian community. The sex offender's past means such involvement needs to include helping him manage his behaviour and not get into situations which in the past led to offences. It also means protecting him from the danger of having false allegations and suspicions levelled at him. We believe that an offender who truly wishes to participate in the life of the church, who realizes the extent of his crime (and the difficulty his presence in the congregation may cause to survivors), and who is truly committed to a new life will understand and accept the need for the imposition of restrictions, even lifelong.

b. The victim's/survivor's perspective

We should start by saying that victims and survivors need exactly the same things from the church as do offenders - acceptance, love, a place to worship and join in fellowship, comrades for the journey, and people who accept her as she is and commit themselves to supporting her in her attempt to live a new life.

Within any church community there may be survivors/victims of the sex offender's crimes. More likely there will be at least some people who are survivors of abuse at the hands of other perpetrators. The minister and other members of the church may not know who they are, as they may not have felt able to tell their story. The long term harm of sexual abuse should not be underestimated, and is often seen most clearly in adult survivors' continuing pain and their struggle to create a sense of self and meaning. Many succeed against the odds (often with little support), many do not. Research suggests that children and adult survivors of abuse want messages from communities which reduce the sense of isolation and blame that they feel. All members of society need to be encouraged to listen to and support children and adults who have been abused. How the Church responds to sex offenders affects them. Survivors in congregations where a sex offender is allowed to participate fully in the life of the church community may feel their own pain has not been acknowledged and heard. It may be very difficult for them to remain as a member of the same congregation; even more difficult to be expected to be in the same housegroup. They may feel they have to leave the congregation or even abandon their faith.

The case was strongly made to the working party that if greater attention appears to be paid to measures relating to restoring the perpetrator than on caring for the victims, this can appear to continue the original inequality that allowed the abuse. While pastoral care of offenders is clearly something Christians must address, pastoral care of survivors has often been ignored or neglected and many survivors have felt alone and abandoned. If sex offending is treated lightly; if a person is quickly restored to positions of trust and authority, this can seem to devalue the significance of a victim's experience.

As stated elsewhere in this report, we believe more work needs to be done on offering effective pastoral care and support to victims and survivors.

c. The church's perspective

Obviously the church, unlike wider society, is committed to being a welcoming, accepting community. No-one is beyond the reach of God's love. So we have a responsibility to bring together people of diverse and sometimes conflicting experience within the same community of love. That is the vision of our calling. It is clearly not that easy. But its difficulty cannot lead us to drop the vision.

Where abuse has occurred within the life of a church, or there have been allegations involving members of that church, there are likely to be divided loyalties and people will find it difficult to know how to deal with these. Many allegations do not lead to prosecution or conviction and the church is left with suspicions and unresolved tensions. Some people, including the one against whom the allegation was made, will see him as having 'been cleared'. Others may believe 'there is no smoke without fire' and be concerned that while the evidence was not sufficient to lead to a conviction, there may be more than sufficient reason to believe that person is not suitable to continue to work with children. Those who pursued the original allegation will be as vulnerable as those who opposed it. If the allegation is not proved their position will be extremely difficult. Such a situation calls for particularly sensitive pastoral support, some of which may need to be provided from elsewhere in the circuit or district. Communities can become deeply divided in such situations.

Great sensitivity, planning and forethought will be required where a church community contains both offenders and survivors and their families. Those responsible, both lay and ordained, may require (and should obtain) specialist advice and assistance in ensuring that the pastoral needs of all are taken seriously and addressed.

d. The wider community's perspective

Within the wider community many known sex offenders find it difficult to rebuild their lives on release from prison. They are not welcome. They may be hounded from one place to another. Nowhere is really safe for them. They are demonized. And the Church cannot condone this way of treating anyone. Indeed, the Church should bear witness to a different approach to all offenders from that of society as a whole. It should welcome their families and enable them to join or remain part of the wider fellowship of the Church. At the same time the Church needs to be seen to stand with vulnerable and abused people, to ensure that victims and survivors are supported and their pastoral needs met, and to do what it can to make life safer for children. For many sex offenders, social isolation and a failure to integrate into an adult community contribute to an emotional lovelessness and poor self-esteem that serve to increase the risk of re-offending. To offer them appropriate support is, at the same time, to further the needs of child protection.

e. The minister's perspective (In many churches, particularly in smaller communities, this will also be the perspective of local preachers, stewards and other church leaders.)

As the one who on Sunday pronounces absolution and preaches forgiveness, a minister is faced with working out what these things mean in practice. The minister may want to help a sex offender become part of the Christian community and grow in faith but there is tension because the minister is also responsible for making sure that boundaries are kept. It is likely to be the minister who receives a phone call from a prison chaplain saying that a sex offender is coming towards the end of his sentence and wants to move to a new area and become part of the life of your local church. But the minister is also trusted by parents, both churchgoers and those who 'send' their children to junior church, shell group or uniformed organization - and those parents would be amazed to discover that you have welcomed a sex offender into the church without warning anyone. But the minister also knows that if you had warned people, many of them are unforgiving and the offender may not have been made welcome.

Evidence we received from circuit ministers suggested it is important for a minister not to be seen as taking sides. In many situations, a minister will therefore need to divide the provision of pastoral support between different people (e.g. where an offender, his victim and his family remain members of the same church it is inadvisable for the same person to try to offer support to all parties). Other ministers, pastoral visitors, colleagues outside the church, members of District Taking Care groups or people appointed as advisors under the new complaints and discipline procedures may all be potential sources of support.

Dealing with these issues can be incredibly emotionally draining. It is essential that good supervision and support are made available and ministers and others are encouraged to take it up. The 1997 Report on Sexual Harassment and Abuse proposed that increased attention should be paid to developing effective supervision of pastoral work and suggested some ways in which this might be done. We believe this is important for effective ministry in general, but especially so in situations such as those discussed in this report, if ministers are to do this work with balance and sensitivity. Circuit Superintendents and District Chairs carry a particular responsibility to seek to ensure such support and supervision is provided. The working party believes this is a very important matter for the Methodist Council to address.

There are particular sensitivities relating to confidentiality and the working party believes the earlier Conference Report on confidentiality is very useful in balancing what is said in pastoral conversations against the need to keep children and young people safe. As the practice of supervision develops, we would also encourage the development of a 'team' approach to confidentiality, where a minister can state 'up front' to an offender that there are limits and that this is to ensure that they are safe, as well as to ensure the safety of others. In developing a multi-agency response to helping sex offenders rebuild their lives, there also needs to be agreement with the offender about types of information to be exchanged between agencies working with him.

7   PRACTICAL IMPLICATIONS

a. Commentary on the Methodist Church's current Safeguarding procedures

The current position in the Methodist Church, under S.O 010 (2), is that

(i)   no person who has been convicted of or has received a formal caution from the police concerning an offence mentioned in the First Schedule to the Children and Young Persons Act 1933 shall undertake work with children and young persons in the life of the Church;

(ii) no person who has been convicted of or has received a formal caution from the police concerning sexual offences against children shall be appointed to any office, post or responsibility or engaged under any contract to which this sub-clause applies.

The working party wish to affirm their support of this Standing Order, for reasons stated in section 5b. of this report.

The working party felt that consideration should be given as to whether there is an anomaly to be addressed in the way we treat sex offenders against adults differently from those who offend against children.

The working part considered how to respond in situations where a convicted or cautioned offender continues to protest his innocence and where some members of the church support his claim. We believe that if a person has been convicted or received an official police caution the church can only work on the basis of that history and not accept a person's story that they were 'framed' as a basis for ignoring the conviction or the caution. While there clearly have been miscarriages of justice in our legal system, there are also cases of guilty people continuing to proclaim their innocence (and of sex offenders minimizing or denying what they did). If the offender believes an injustice has been done there are appropriate ways forward, to seek to have the conviction overturned and their name formally cleared. Until such time as that happens, the church has to work with the record as it exists.

b. Procedures necessary for offenders to be involved in a church community

The notice of motion describes the church as '*a community of love, forgiveness and reconciliation, committed to the restoration of broken people and communities.*' It clearly has a role to play in offering pastoral support and care to those in the local church and community who have committed sexual offences. What is more, a relatively high proportion of sex offenders have been involved in the life and worship of the prison chapel and would hope to continue their involvement in Christian worship and fellowship on release. Indeed, many sex offenders see the church as having a significant part to play in helping them rebuild their lives. Like everyone else, such offenders have much both to receive and contribute within the life of a local church community and their participation in the worship and fellowship of a local church enables faith to grow and develop. For the protection of the church community, survivors, and particularly children and young people, but also for the protection of the offender (who needs not to be put in situations where he could be vulnerable to accusation or to the opportunity to reoffend) it will be important that the basis of their involvement in a local church is clearly understood and stated.

We suggest Methodist churches should adopt the following procedure:

i. Pre-release

Where the offender is approaching release from prison, it will be important wherever possible for the chaplain of the prison to be in contact with the minister of the local church and circuit where the offender hopes to settle on release. If the circuit minister is aware of the arrival of a sex offender but has not heard from the prison chaplain, the minister should try to make contact with the chaplain, who may be able to describe the treatment received by the offender and the kind of programme that will be in place to help him return to the community. It may be possible for a visit to be arranged so that the minister can meet the chaplain and the offender. It will also be crucial for those responsible in the local church to be in contact with the local risk management panel, the offender's probation officer and the police, so that any agreement regarding involvement in the local church is known about and seen as part of the multi-agency, multi-disciplinary approach to the oversight of the offender upon release from prison. In approaching and seeking to work with secular agencies there may be some initial suspicion and it may help to provide the agency with a copy of the Methodist Church's procedure or even this whole report, to demonstrate the Church's willingness to work together with other agencies in the responsibility for sex offenders and the protection of potential victims. (See Resolution 38/3(b).)

For known sex offenders already living in the community and involved in the life of the church, the same provisions should be made.

ii. Setting up a small group within the church

A small group should be set up, consisting of approximately five persons, including the minister, persons who have agreed to offer pastoral support for the offender and accompany them in worship and other church activities, someone with expertise or experience in this field and someone to represent the wider church community. The group should acquaint itself with any therapeutic programme the offender has undergone or will continue to be part of. The group should meet the offender, their probation officer and other appropriate people so that clear boundaries can be established for the protection of children and young people and to reduce the likelihood of false allegations or suspicions. This group will, at best, operate alongside other agencies in a multi-agency approach to the offender's rehabilitation.

iii. Carrying out a risk assessment

One of the first tasks of the small group will be to carry out a risk assessment. This will involve looking at the church building and activities with a view to identifying potential risks that will need to be guarded against or which could lead to the offender being vulnerable to allegations. The offender's probation officer or another member of the risk management panel may be willing to help with this assessment as part of their arrangements for the offender. Having identified the potential risks the group needs to consider how they can be minimized either by a change in practice or by monitoring or restricting the offender's participation in any particular activities. The results of the risk assessment will lead to the creation of an agreed 'contract' with the offender.

iv. Writing a contract

When the boundaries and terms of involvement have been discussed and agreed with the offender, they should be written into a contract (see below). While a written contract sounds very formal, sex offenders can be manipulative and test boundaries. A written contract clarifies the terms on which the person is involved in the life of the church. The contract should involve the person's family and partner who may also be attending church and need to be informed. It might begin by setting out the pastoral support and care being offered by the church and then move on to other conditions, such as some of the following examples:

* I will never allow myself to be in a situation where I am alone with children/young people
* I will attend meetings/house groups as directed by the small group
* I will sit where directed in the church and will not place myself in the vicinity of children and young people

* I will not enter certain parts of the building designated by the small group, nor any area where children's activities are in progress

* I will decline invitations of hospitality where there are children in the home

* I accept that 'x' and 'y' will sit with me during church activities, accompanying me when I need to use other facilities. They will know that I am a Schedule 1 offender/registered with the police under the terms of the Sex Offenders Act

* I accept that 'z' will provide me with pastoral care

* I accept that there are certain people who will need to be told of my circumstances in order for them to protect the children/young people for whom they care

* I accept that contact will need to be made with my probation officer, who will meet with church leaders or members of the small group as and when necessary

* I understand that if I do not keep to these conditions, then I may be banned from attending the church, and in such circumstances the church leaders may choose to inform the statutory agencies (eg probation and social services) and any other relevant organisation, and the church congregation

* I understand that any other concerns will be taken seriously and reported

* I understand that this contract will be reviewed regularly every _____ months and will remain for an indefinite period.

(adapted from *Guidance to Churches: protecting children and appointing children's workers*, Churches Child Protection Advisory Service)

The document needs to be signed and dated by the offender and by the church representatives.

v. *Small group to meet regularly*

The small group should continue to meet the individual from time to time to review the arrangement and address any concerns. If boundaries are not being kept, or if the contract is not being kept in other ways, it is important to address the problem. (In extreme cases, where boundaries continue not to be kept, it may be necessary to prohibit the offender from coming on the premises.) When officers or ministers change in the church it will be important to ensure continuity of awareness and provision of pastoral support for the offender.

vi. *Making people aware - who needs to know what?*

A sex offender coming to join a congregation may not want people to know his history. One of the important matters for the small group and the offender will be an agreement on who needs to know. Without agreement on this, it will not be possible for the offender to join the congregation. Key people, especially those responsible for leading children's and young people's groups, need to know that the person is attending the church, that he should not be having contact with the children and that he should never be on his own with children and young people.

There is much to be said for explaining the circumstances to the whole congregation, to promote understanding and support for the individual but also to ensure that church members do not unwittingly allow children contact with the individual concerned. However, this needs to be weighed against any need for confidentiality or pastoral sensitivity. It will be important to obtain advice from the statutory agencies and the risk management panel. The need to know must be balanced with the danger that the offender may be hounded out of the community (to his detriment and to the greater danger of other children if he decides to maintain a lower profile next time around).

Always we should promote awareness within the church of what would happen if a sex offender joined the congregation. It could be explained that from time to time this might happen and, if it does, then the procedures are as described in this report (i.e. that people who need to know because they work with children in the church are informed; the church liaises with other concerned agencies; a small group will link with the offender; there will be a contract; arrangements will be reviewed regularly.) This information is particularly important to survivors. They are likely to ask (and need to know) how they will be kept safe. Who can they go and talk to if they feel frightened, worried or hurt?

c. General points

i. *Young offenders*

Approximately one third of sex offenders are adolescents. With young offenders, as with adults, the church needs to liaise with the risk management panel and look at how to reduce future risk. The young offender will need to sign a contract and so will those with parental responsibility for them.

ii. *Developing good practice*

The general need for the Church to adopt good practice in child protection terms cannot be over-emphasized. Adopting the Safeguarding procedures both helps deal with known offenders and offers the best possible safeguard against the activities of offenders who are not known about and who have not been caught.

Support

The nature of sexual abuse and offending is such as to raise very emotional and difficult situations that can be stressful for all. It is important for those with responsibilities to have appropriate support networks. One of these networks is likely to include members of other agencies with responsibilities for sex offenders in the community (especially Police and Probation). Another will be within the church, where there is developing experience and expertise in this area of work. Each District should develop a team of those who can offer consultancy and support where necessary (including members of a Taking Care group where there is one, Training and Development Officer, Child Protection Officer, etc.)

8 MEMBERS OF THE WORKING PARTY

Richard G Jones (chair)	Pearl Luxon
Paul Beetham	Elizabeth Ovey (from September 1999)
Andrew Cordy	Pennie Pennie
Anne Hollows	Caroline Riley (from September 1999)
Shaun Kelly	David Gamble (convenor)

9 RESOLUTIONS

38/1. The Conference adopts the report and resolves that it shall constitute the reply to Memorials M45 and M46 of 1999.

38/2. The Conference:

(a) reaffirms its commitment to the creation of a community of love, forgiveness and reconciliation and to the restoration of broken people and communities;

(b) recognizes that in making that commitment effective it must be sensitive both to the feelings and needs of existing and potential sufferers from abuse and sexual crime and to the needs of offenders and their families, to all of whom it will seek to offer appropriate and informed pastoral support and care;

(c) reaffirms its belief that the current Safeguarding procedures of the Methodist Church are in the interests of both children and young people and of individuals within the Church who have in the past been convicted of or received a formal caution in respect of sexual offences;

(d) believes that the needs of child protection and of pastoral support for persons so convicted or cautioned should be seen as complementary rather than as matters to be dealt with separately in the life of the Church.

38/3. The Conference directs that:

(a) the procedure set out in section 7b of the report be adopted as the practice of the Methodist Church when a person who has been convicted of or has received a formal caution in respect of a sexual offence seeks to become part of a local church community;

(b) it be referred to the connexional Team for consideration of how that procedure may be published for use in the Church and in a form which can be made available to risk management panels, probation services, the police and other agencies;

(c) it be referred to the Superintendent Chaplain of Prisons to consider in consultation with those persons appointed as Methodist chaplains in pastoral care of inmates of prisons and prison staff whether there are improvements to be made in the way in which such chaplains relate to local churches and circuits over the release of prisoners convicted of sexual offences into local communities, how such prisoners can be prepared for their involvement in churches following the procedure set out in this report, and whether there are means by which the wider Church community may be enabled better to understand the work done by and the concerns of such chaplains;

(d) all those in training for ordained ministry in the Methodist Church should receive training in child protection and the rehabilitation of persons so convicted or cautioned within the life of the Church.

38/4. The Conference refers to the Methodist Council for consideration:

(a) the possibility of establishing a further working party or determining some other way, preferably in consultation with other Churches, to consider how pastoral care and support may most effectively be offered to survivors of sexual abuse;

(b) the implications of the report for structures for support and supervision at circuit and district level; special attention should be given to the provision of support for those involved in situations in which a person who has been convicted of or received a formal caution in respect of a sexual offence is seeking to or has become part of a local church community;

(c) whether it is anomalous that the Church distinguishes in its treatment of persons so convicted or cautioned by reference to the question whether the offence was or offences were committed against an adult or against a child or young person, and if so, by what means that anomaly might be addressed;

(d) how training and awareness-building relating to the issues raised in the report might be offered.

(e) whether

   (i) the procedures set out in section 7b require to be incorporated in Standing Orders and

   (ii) in exceptional circumstances the Senior Persons Group should have power to authorise a local church to dispense with following that procedure

   and to bring a report to the Conference of 2001 with any amendments to Standing Orders which may be proposed as a result of that consideration.

38/5. The Conference directs the Methodist Council to bring to the Conference of 2001 for its judgment amendments to Standing Orders, such that in the exceptional circumstances outlined in the report the Senior Persons' Group which now considers and advises upon cases of ministers and local preachers who have been so convicted or cautioned shall have power to determine that a person so convicted or cautioned, whether presbyteral, diaconal or lay, should be eligible to hold office in the Church notwithstanding the provisions of Standing Order 010(2).

38/6. The Conference directs the Methodist Council to review the developments in the life of the Church which follow from the report and to report on those developments to the Conference of 2003.

APPENDIX A HISTORY AND BACKGROUND OF THE REPORT

This report has been produced by a working party set up in response to a Notice of Motion adopted by the Methodist Conference in 1997:

Notice of Motion No 10, Sexual Offences: Subsequent pastoral care:

The Conference directs the Methodist Council to establish a working group with relevant expertise and experience to consider the ways in which appropriate and informed pastoral support and care may be given to those in the local church and community who have committed sexual offences, and to bring specific recommendations to the Conference of 1998.

The Conference does this, recognising that as a community of love, forgiveness and reconciliation, committed to the restoration of broken people and communities, it must be sensitive to the feelings and needs of existing and potential sufferers from abuse, as well as the needs of offenders.

The Methodist Council referred this matter to the Working Party on Sexual Harassment and Abuse. Following discussions in the working party and at an ecumenical seminar held at Leyhill Prison on March 26th 1998, this working party was set up with the following amended terms of reference:

1. *To consider the ways in which appropriate and informed pastoral support and care may be given to those in the local church and community who have committed sexual offences*

2. *To listen to and learn from the experience of those individuals and communities most closely involved in this issue, particularly offenders, victims and their families, and representatives of local churches with relevant experience*

3. *To consult and co-operate with other churches, agencies and individuals engaged in this field*

4. *To report and make specific recommendations in the first instance to the Methodist Council, and then to the Methodist Conference in 1999.*

The Background – The Safeguarding procedures and notices of motion

For a number of years during the 1990s, Conference had been asked to deal with issues relating to child protection, following the publication of the Home Office's Safe from Harm Guidelines and the Methodist Division of Education and Youth's Safeguarding procedures and booklets. Particular care was to be taken in the appointment of workers with children and young people. However, experience within the church community made it clear that due care had to be taken in the making of all appointments. Standing Orders were amended to include the following requirement (as amended in 1999):

010 Qualification for Appointment

(2) Subject to the provisions of the Rehabilitation of Offenders Act 1974 (or any statutory modification or re-enactment thereof for the time being in force and any regulations or orders made or having effect thereunder)

(i) no person who has been convicted of or has received a formal caution from the police concerning an offence mentioned in the First Schedule to the Children and Young Persons Act 1933 shall undertake work with children and young persons in the life of the Church;

(ii) no person who has been convicted of or has received a formal caution from the police concerning sexual offences against children shall be appointed to any office, post or responsibility or engaged under any contract to which this sub-clause applies

(3) Sub-clause (ii) of clause (2) above shall apply to:

(iii) first appointment to a station as a ministerial or diaconal probationer or, if no such appointment has been made, admission into full connexion as a minister or deacon;

(iv) first appointment to a station as a minister or deacon recognised and regarded as such under the Deed of Union or first entry upon the stations as a minister or deacon authorised by the Conference to serve as such

(v) readmission into full connexion as a minister or deacon;

(vi) any other appointment or re-appointment to any office, post or responsibility or any engagement or re-engagement under a contract of service or for services which is at the date of appointment, re-appointment, engagement or re-engagement specified for this purpose by the Methodist Council, either generally by reference to categories or by a ruling in the particular case.

(4) Clause (2) above shall have effect in relation to persons in any jurisdiction within the home Districts other than England and Wales as if, in any such jurisdiction in which any of the legislative provisions there mentioned does not have effect, there were substituted a reference to the legislation, if any, of similar substance in force in that jurisdiction from time to time.

In response to clause 3 (vi), later in 1999 the Methodist Council agreed the following categories:

1 Any duty or responsibility exercised on behalf of the Methodist Church which involves:

a. lone access to church premises

b. face-to-face contact with children and young people without the presence of another adult

c. carrying out duties off church premises in circumstances in which the person concerned may be seen as a representative of the church.

2. Any office within the following categories:

Representational membership of the	**Liturgical or pastoral**
Church Council	Local Preachers
Circuit Meeting	Worship leaders
District Synod	Organists/choir leaders
Methodist Council	Pastoral visitors/Class leaders
Methodist Conference	Workers with children and young people

In the light of what was beginning to look like a life-long, blanket ban on sex offenders holding office in the church, the 1997 Notice of Motion sought to ensure that due consideration was given to their place in the church and to the provision of appropriate pastoral support and care for them. The 1999 Conference referred two memorials to the working party, each expressing unease at the apparent inflexibility of the new S.O. 010.

Two further memorials, from the 1999 Conference, were referred to the working party:

M45 SAFEGUARDING CHILDREN AND YOUNG PEOPLE (1)

The Nottingham (North) (22/1) Circuit Meeting (Present: 40. Vote: Unan.) recognises the importance of safeguarding children and young people, but feels that Standing Order 010 section 2 (ii) presents a requirement which is unnecessary and contrary to our Church's doctrines.

In our view, it is unnecessary because many holders of offices within the Church have no contact with children. Attendance at church services when children are present can give a greater contact with children and the holding of office per se.

Our theological problem with the Standing Order is over its apparent disregard for the doctrine of forgiveness and restitution which is at the heart of the doctrines which the same Standing Order states must be upheld.

The Nottingham North Circuit requests that, either:

1. S.O. 010 Section 2 (ii) be redrafted to deal with the theological qualifications referred to above; or,

2. A considered statement be issued as a matter of urgency explaining the answers to the theological reservations raised, in order to allay the serious disquiet felt by people - both lay and ordained - within this Circuit.

M46 SAFEGUARDING CHILDREN AND YOUNG PEOPLE (2)

The Saltash (12/22) Circuit Meeting (Present: 32. Vote: 29 for, 0 ag) recognises and appreciates the importance of providing the utmost protection to children and of the issues addressed in standing Order 010 (2), but believe that, in its present form, this Standing Order leaves the church wide open to serious criticism. The meeting, therefore, requests the Conference to consider the following three comments and the two proposals that flow therefrom.

1. *The standing order allows for no exceptions. Yet both Scripture and the history of the church bear witness to the fact that God can and will overturn human regulations and restrictions to 'Call' whom he wills into service.* **It is our conviction that the church should take account of judgements made by Civil Courts and the Police but not in such a way as to deny room for the working of God the Holy Spirit.**

2. *The Order provides no opportunity for persons previously convicted or in receipt of a formal Police Caution to relate those past events to their present life and service in the membership of God's People. We draw attention to the fact that not all Court Convictions or Police Cautions are 'Infallible' or 'Safe', nor do they all bear the same weight. (A married man of 40, convicted at the age of 18 of having sexual intercourse with a minor, is not inevitably thereby a dangerous person to his own children or that of others).* **It is our conviction that the love of God requires the church always to exercise (and to be seen as exercising) personal judgement rather than imposing an impersonal blanket exclusion based solely on the judgement of secular authorities.**

3. *The Order prohibits those described from being appointed to 'Office' in the life of the church. Since, however, the word 'Office' is not defined except as that which requires the formality of 'appointment', the application of this Order is open to varied interpretation.* **It is our conviction that in so sensitive an area of church life, a lack of definition in regard to the word 'Office' will lead to bitterness and division between both local churches and circuits.**

Proposal One:
The Conference establish a 'Judicial' (or otherwise named) Committee in each District, so that any person with a previous conviction or caution as defined in the current S.O. 010 (2) (i and ii), but who now personally affirms a 'Call to Serve' and locally is deemed worthy of appointment, may be tested and adjudged. In the event of such a Committee being established, paragraphs (i and ii) would require the addition of the sentence **'unless approval has been granted by the District "Judicial" Committee'.**

Proposal Two:
The Conference provide a precise clarification of the term 'Office' in S.O. 010 (2) (ii). (This proposal was the subject of an amendment to Standing Orders brought by the Law and Polity Committee.)

APPENDIX B THE SURVEY OF MINISTERS

Seven questions were asked and the returns were as follows (the answers to the 7th question have not been added to the table):

(in the chart 5/6 means 5 ministers reported 6 cases)

		Chester & Stoke	London NW	S Wales	N Wales	Cymru	Total
1	In your current appointment how many adults do you know who have a history of sexual offending against children?	5/6	6/10	1/1	6/9	1/2	19/28
2	How many of the offenders have returned to a church where they were already known?	4/4	2/2	0/0	3/3	–	9/9
3	How many were referred, having been unknown before?	1/1	1/1	0/0	0/0	–	2/2
4	How many just arrived?	0/0	1/1	0/0	2/2	–	3/3
5	Again, in your current appointment, how many children do you know who have been the victims of such offending?	children 2/5 adults 2/4	children 6/8 adults 2/22	children 2/4 adults 1/2	children 3/5 adults 1/several	–	13/22 5/28+
6	How many instances of sexual offenders becoming part of your church have you known in your previous appointments?	7/8	5/11	2/4	10/15	4/5	28/43
7	How long have you been in the Circuit work?						
	TOTAL QUESTIONNAIRES RETURNED	46	30	24	24	19	143

APPENDIX C

The following list is that published in *Safeguarding: A policy for good practice in the care of children and young people* (2000). Because the Church's Safeguarding procedures relate specifically to child protection, it is a list of sexual offences against children. Anyone with a conviction or official police caution for any of these offences is prohibited from holding office within the Methodist Church (See Appendix A). The current report raises the issue of the anomaly with regard to offenders against adults.

SAFEGUARDING FORM B. LIST OF OFFENCES

Sexual offences which, if committed against a person under the age of 18 (in cases in which the offence may also be committed against an adult), bar people from holding office in England and Wales

1   An offence under Section 1 of the Sexual Offences Act 1956 (rape) when committed against a person under the age of 18.

2   An offence specified in Schedule 1 to the Children and Young Persons Act 1933, namely:

a   Children and Young Persons Act 1933

Section 3   Allowing persons under sixteen to be in brothels

b. Sexual Offences Act 1956

Sections 2&3	Procurement of intercourse by threats or false imprisonment
Section 4	Administering drugs to obtain or facilitate intercourse
Section 5	Sexual intercourse with a girl under 13
Section 6	Sexual intercourse with a girl under 16
Sections 7&9	Intercourse with defectives
Section 10	Incest by a man
Section 11	Incest by a woman
Section 12	Buggery
Section 13	Gross indecency
Section 14	Indecent assault on a man
Section 15	Indecent assault on a woman
Section 16	Assault with intention to commit buggery
Section 19	Abduction of unmarried girl under 18 from parent or guardian
Section 20	Abduction of unmarried girl under 16 from parent or guardian
Section 22	Causing prostitution of women
Section 23	Procuration of a girl under 21
Section 24	Detention of a woman in a brothel or other premises
Sections 25 & 26	Allowing premises to be used for intercourse
Section 28	Causing or encouraging prostitution etc.

3   An offence under section 1(1) of the Indecency with Children Act 1960 (indecent conduct towards a child)

4   An offence under section 54 of the Criminal Law Act 1977 (inciting a girl under 16 to have incestuous sexual intercourse)

5   An offence contrary to section 1 of the Protection of Children Act 1978 (indecent photographs of children)

6   An offence contrary to section 160 of the Criminal Justice Act 1988 (the possession of indecent photographs of children)

7   An offence contrary to section 170 of the Customs and Excise Management Act 1979 in relation to goods prohibited to be imported under section 42 of the Customs Consolidation Act 1876 (prohibitions and restrictions relating to pornography) where the prohibited goods included indecent photographs of children under the age of 16.

Sexual Offences which bar people from holding office in Scotland

1   An offence of rape (when committed against a person under the age of 18)

2   An offence specified in Schedule 1 to the Criminal Procedure (Scotland) Act 1995

3   An offence contrary to section 170 of the Customs and Excise Management Act 1979 in relation to goods prohibited to be imported under Section 42 of the Customs Consolidation Act 1876 (prohibitions and restrictions relating to pornography) where the prohibited goods included indecent photographs of children under the age of 16

4   An offence under sections 52 and 52A of the Civic Government (Scotland) Act 1982 (indecent photographs)

NB.   Within other legal jurisdictions, SO 010 (4) states that the restriction on holding office 'shall have effect in relation to persons in any jurisdiction within the home Districts other than England and Wales as if, in any such jurisdiction in which any of the legislative provisions there mentioned does not have effect, there were substituted a reference to the legislation, if any, of similar substance in force in that jurisdiction from time to time.'

APPENDIX D ADDITIONAL MATERIAL FOR USE WHEN STUDYING THIS REPORT IN CHURCH GROUPS

1 A Biblical way into the report

Matthew 18 is very challenging in relation to the issues raised in this report.

Divide the chapter into sections: verses 1-7; 8-11; 12-14; 15-20; 21-35.

Allocate each section to an individual or small group and allow about 5 minutes for them to reflect on their section, asking the question - What is this passage saying about the issues raised in this report?

Then share findings.

2 A Litany
(from Richard Jones, used at a meeting of the Working Party)

Let us thank God for human sexuality and all its energies -

> inspiring so much creativity
> giving vitality to human communities
> enabling partnerships to find strength and commitment
> enabling new births to come to be
> enriching family life

Let us confess our sins -

> Wherein we have made sexuality:
> a weapon to exploit others or manipulate the weak
> a vehicle for lust or exhibitionism
> a means to satisfy our own selfishness
> or wherein we have been impure, unforgiving or uncaring
> **Good Lord, have mercy on us**

Let us pray for:

Those who long for rewarding human relationships and have never experienced them
> **Lord have mercy**

Those whose sexual life is constant fantasy
> **Lord have mercy**

Those whose families have fallen apart
> **Lord have mercy**

Those who are orphaned or have no caring home
> **Lord have mercy**

Those who are bruised or bewildered by failed marriages or partnerships
> **Lord have mercy**

Those who long for children but cannot have them
> **Lord have mercy**

Those who have been traumatised by sexual abuse
> **Lord have mercy**

Those who have committed sexual offences, whether or not they have been found out
Lord have mercy
Those who care professionally for sexual offenders and their rehabilitation
Lord have mercy
Those whose friends or partners are in prison for sexual offences
Lord have mercy
Congregations caring for sexual offenders who have joined them
Lord have mercy

In the name of Christ
Amen

APPENDIX E   A SHORT LIST OF RESOURCES

Good Practice Guides

Good Practice, The United Reformed Church, 1998/99

Guidance to Churches: Protecting Children and appointing children's workers, PCCA, 1998

Meeting the Challenge - How churches should respond to sex offenders, Church of England Board for Social Responsibility, 1999

Safeguarding: A policy for good practice in the care of children and young people, The Methodist Church, 2000

Related books

Cashman, H. *Christianity and Child Sexual Abuse*, SPCK, 1993

Grubin, D. *Sex Offending against children; Understanding the risk*, Police Research Series Paper 99, 1998

Kennedy, M. *The Courage to tell; Christian survivors of sexual abuse tell their stories of pain and hope*, Churches Together in Britain and Ireland, 1999

Moule, C. F. D. *Forgiveness and Reconciliation*, SPCK, 1999

Parkinson, P. *Child Sexual Abuse and the Churches*, Hodder and Stoughton, 1997

Poling, James Newton, *The Abuse of Power: A Theological problem*, Abingdon, 1991

Tutu, D. *No future without forgiveness*, Rider, 1999

Children and Holy Communion

1 INTRODUCTION

1.1 The 1987 Guidelines

The Methodist Conference has for many years been concerned with the issue of Children and Communion. Two interim reports were considered in the 1970s. The Conference of 1987 adopted the report *Children in Communion*. Its central recommendations were presented in the form of Guidelines for the use of local churches. These Guidelines remain in place. Whilst acknowledging that the final responsibility for what happens in the local church remains with the Church Council, the adopted Report expressed the conviction that *'the time has come to move forward and encourage children to participate fully in the Lord's Supper.'*

1.2 Practice in other churches

Children and Communion is not an issue for the Methodist Church alone. The recent report *Baptism and Church Membership* (Churches Together in England) highlights other ways in which the issues have been addressed. Due account should be taken of this, especially bearing in mind the large number of Local Ecumenical Partnerships [LEPs] in which Methodism shares, in particular with the United Reformed Church and with the Church of England. Alongside this it should be noted that in churches which are not LEPs there will also be people from different denominations and backgrounds (see Section 4).

1.3 Remit of the Working Group

Ten years after *Children in Communion*, a Working Party was given a remit from the then Division of Education and Youth to look at the practice of Methodist churches in the matter of admitting children to Holy Communion. The remit noted that 'there is inconsistency in the interpretation of the guidelines in the 1987 Report and therefore the practice of churches. There is also development in the practice of other churches, with some of whom Methodism has inter-Communion and shared life in LEPs.' The task of the Working Party was **'to discover what is happening, particularly in the Methodist Church in Britain, and to help the church to address this issue.'**

1.4 What the Group did

The Working Group decided to discover present practice in Methodist churches (including LEPs in which Methodists share) by a direct approach rather than by anecdotal evidence and commissioned a survey to gather this information. The main findings are presented in this Report. In the light of this information and other developments which have occurred within both the Methodist church and other traditions a number of issues have been identified. **It is recommended that the 1987 Guidelines be replaced by the policy set out at the end of this Report.**

2   THE SURVEY

2.1   Research Method

In the summer of 1997 a fully structured self-completion postal questionnaire was sent to a representative sample of ministers in pastoral charge of churches across the connexion. The sample was drawn from the annual statistical data returned through circuits and districts. In order to minimize enquiries of churches with no children those returning five or fewer present in Junior Church were excluded from the sampling frame - reducing its size by 46%. Ministers were asked to complete the questionnaire only with the specified church in their section in mind, thereby ensuring that smaller churches as well as larger ones featured in the research. Where necessary, a reminder letter was sent to encourage ministers to complete the questionnaire. 324 out of 390 ministers replied to the survey - an excellent response rate of 83%. It transpired that some 18% of the churches covered by the survey indicated that they had five children or fewer in their Junior Church when the time came to complete the questionnaire which means that the experience of churches with a small number of children was represented in the survey.

2.2   Results

2.2.1   Introducing the Policy

2.2.1.1   Is there a *Children in Communion* policy in place?

69% of Church Councils which were sampled had discussed children in Communion and 56% had agreed a formal policy. Where a policy had not been agreed a further 21% of churches had an informal policy which had not been the subject of Church Council discussion. If this figure is added to the 56% of Church Councils with an agreed policy then 77% of the churches sampled claim to have a policy of some kind.

2.2.1.2   *What policy is in place?*

83% of churches with a policy for children in Communion are offering children the elements either conditionally [43%] or unconditionally [40%].

2.2.1.3   *Who took the initiative for setting the policy?*

Minister	73%
Junior Church Staff	38%
Church Council	11%
Parents	11%

Base: churches with a policy – more than one answer possible

2.2.1.4   What reservations did churches have about the introduction of the Policy?

Just over a third of churches had reservations about introducing a policy. In order of importance those identified from a given list were:

> Children would not know what is going on
> Children would lack proper reverence

We had to wait until we were Church Members to receive Communion and so should the children
The children would disrupt the atmosphere
Base: churches with a policy where reservations were expressed.

2.2.1.5 How was the policy received initially within the church?

Broad acceptance	70%
Significant reservations which were resolved	10%
Significant reservations which persist	5%
Don't know	15% *

Base: churches where children can receive elements either conditionally or unconditionally.

* High because minister may not have been in pastoral charge at time of decision.

2.2.1.6 What impact did the introduction of the policy have on the congregation?

In order of importance the following benefits were noted from a list provided in the questionnaire:

Encouraged people to think more deeply about matters relating to children in the church	51%
Brought the church family closer together	47%
Children have been made more welcome at worship	45%
Encouraged wider participation in worship	37%
It's as if we have always been doing it	35%
Adults have been helped to think more deeply about the place of Holy Communion in their own life	29%
Sharpened divisions between those for and against	1%

Base: churches where children can receive elements either conditionally or unconditionally.

2.2.1.7 What measures were thought to be important in the introduction of the policy?

The percentage of ministers identifying the following measures as important or very important from a given list was as follows:

Preparation of children in Junior Church groups	67%
Church Council decided on a policy to allow children to receive the elements	60%
Minister talking to the children by themselves	42%
Pastoral preaching to explain the reasons for the decision	40%
Discussion at Worship Consultation	35%
Letter to parents to explain policy	32%

Base: churches where children can receive elements either conditionally or unconditionally – more than one answer possible.

2.2.2   Church Practice

2.2.2.1   *When are children present at some point during the service of Holy Communion?*

Every time Communion is celebrated	43%)	
Most times when Communion is celebrated	21%)	87%
Family Communions only	23%)	
Never	13%	

Base: all churches sampled.

2.2.2.2   *Which parts of the service are children present for?*

	'Normal' Communion	Family Communion Service
All of it including the distribution of elements	13%	85%
Only present at the end of worship when the elements are distributed	30%	9%
All except for the middle of the service	21%	6%
Start of worship but not for distribution of elements	36%	nil

Base: where children are present

2.2.2.3   *Where a family Communion is celebrated which service books are used?*

Sunday Service – adult book	61%
Sunday Service – children's book	31%
Other published material	34%
Own liturgy	45%

More than one answer possible.

2.2.2.4   *At what age do children share in different aspects of the service?*

	Under 5	6-7	8-11	12-14
Present but do not come forward	nil	nil	nil	nil
Receive a blessing	55%	35%	22%	10%
Receive elements subject to conditions	15%	32%	43%	42%
Receive unconditionally	14%	20%	22%	25%
Not stated	16%	13%	13%	23%

Base: where children are present when the elements are distributed.

2.2.2.5 Where conditions are specified before the elements are offered – what are they?

	All	LEPs
Child must be baptized	17%	46%
Parents must have given consent/not objected	67%	69%
Child must have indicated a desire to receive	80%	77%
Child must have received teaching	63%	54%

Base: Where conditions are applied – more than one answer possible.

2.2.2.6 What is the practice for administering the elements?

Receive with their parents	67%
When parents are not present children receive with adult(s)	53%
Junior Church including staff receive together	55%
Children without parents present receive together	14%

Base: where children may receive the elements. More than one answer possible.

3 DISCUSSION OF ISSUES ARISING FROM THE SURVEY AND OTHER DEVELOPMENTS

The major findings of the survey were reported to the Methodist Council and to the Faith and Order Committee in 1998. Members were invited to reflect upon the implications of the results. In the light of that consultation process and other developments that have occurred since the Guidelines were introduced thirteen years ago, the following issues were identified.

3.1 Diversity – connexionalism or congregationalism

The survey reports a very wide diversity of policy and practice. The 1987 Guidelines place the final responsibility for what happens in the local church with the Church Council. However, nearly a quarter of churches with six or more children present in church on a Sunday morning have not even discussed the policy issue of children in Communion. It must also be recognised that this approach has made possible a diversity of practice that the church now has to address. The 1987 Guidelines have encouraged a congregational rather than connexional approach to what is an important theological and pastoral matter. Some churches do not have children present at any time during the service of Holy Communion whilst others allow children under the age of five to receive the elements without any condition. This wide variation causes difficulties for families and local churches and is clearly at odds with our connexional ethos.

3.2 The importance of uniform practice across the connexion

Only just over half of those churches with six or more children in their Junior Church have a Children in Communion policy which has been agreed by the Church Council. A further quarter of churches claim to have a *de facto* policy, arising usually out of the particular stance of their current minister.

The absence of a formal policy places children in a situation of uncertainty, especially when pastoral oversight changes or when they themselves are visitors in another Methodist church. The 1987 Report expressed the conviction that the time had come to move forward and encourage children to participate fully in the Lord's Supper. The evidence of the survey is that in the thirteen years since then, this has happened to a large extent. The consequences of the diversity of practice in relation to the 1987 guidelines, however, make it necessary to take seriously one of the three possible ways forward:

1. that the Methodist Church abandon any attempt to offer connexional guidelines;
2. that the present policies be left in place [with or without minor changes];
3. that the Conference agree a policy in relation to children and Holy Communion which applies to the whole connexion.

> Having given due consideration to the results of the survey and having consulted with the Faith and Order Committee, the Methodist Council invites the Conference to adopt the third option.

3.3 The positive experience of introducing Children in Communion

The vast majority of churches report positive experiences from the introduction of the policy. The table at 2.2.1.6 shows that the life of the local church will be enriched and adults helped to think more deeply about the place of Holy Communion in their own spirituality. This should encourage churches across the connexion to include children in Holy Communion and to adopt a positive attitude with regard to their inclusion.

3.4 Conditions to receiving Holy Communion

3.4.1 Open Table ?

Many Methodist churches consider themselves to have 'an open Table' and welcome 'all those who love the Lord Jesus Christ', offering bread and wine to those who come with hands outstretched. God's blessing is proclaimed to those who come but do not wish, for whatever reason, to receive the elements [see para 3.6 below]. God's love for both adults and children, for every human being, is demonstrated by the inclusive act of laying hands upon their head, accompanied by appropriate words. It must be acknowledged that the invitation "to all those who love the Lord Jesus Christ" is not historic Methodist practice. At the same time it is very widespread in the modern Church and also has the intention of being inclusive. It might be proper to ask whether or not it is an acceptable development within the life of the Methodist Church. The rightness of it should not be argued solely on the grounds that its practice is widespread. It might be argued out of a desire to be appropriately inclusive. Nevertheless, the invitation is not all-inclusive and unconditional. It offers a criterion by which women and men may judge whether or not they may or may not present themselves at the Lord's Table. 'Love of the Lord Jesus Christ' would permit the participation of people of other denominational traditions with the additional assumption that they are in good standing in their own Church. It would permit the participation and inclusion of those whose mental powers do not allow them to make any rational decision about it for themselves, a decision on their behalf being taken by those who know and love them.

It is undoubtedly true that children are as capable as adults of being included among 'those who love the Lord Jesus Christ'. But other criteria – age, understanding, preparation and parental consent – are regarded by some as prerequisites before children may receive bread and wine. These are discussed below. First, however, it must be asked whether, for children and adults alike, baptism is a precondition for receiving Communion.

3.4.2 Baptism

The 1987 Guidelines state, as a theological principle, that for a child to be admitted to communicant participation in the Lord's Supper he or she will have been baptized. Where it is discovered that a child has not been baptized, it is expected that after due preparation, baptism will follow. The survey shows that only a small minority of churches make baptism a pre-condition of receiving the elements. Local Ecumenical Partnerships are more likely to impose baptism as a condition. Current practice is at odds with the existing 1987 Guidelines. Baptism remains the rite of entry into the Church and where a child has not been baptized but receives Communion, then baptism should follow as a proper corollary. At present the Church sets out a pattern of Christian initiation that begins with baptism and leads to admission to Holy Communion. In Methodist practice confirmation and reception into membership may take place before or after first Communion. Because in this whole area we are dealing with *a whole process of initiation*, which includes several separable elements, some would argue that provided that the person benefits from both baptism and Holy Communion it does not matter which comes first. The weight of the argument below is, however, that baptism should be required *before* a person receives Holy Communion.

3.4.2.a Holy Communion is by many considered to be a converting ordinance, so that, for some children and adults, the initial reception of Communion in an unbaptized state might well include the desire to be baptized also. If someone were to present himself or herself at the Lord's Table with hands outstretched, the presiding minister knowing this person not to be baptized, this would not be the moment to withhold bread and wine, but it ought immediately to occasion a pastoral conversation to discuss the significance and the consequences of what has happened. This scenario is more likely to apply to adults than to children, but would apply equally well if children, known not to be baptized, were to present themselves with open hands. In the case of children the pastoral conversation would need also to include their parents, whatever the parents' relationship with the Church might be [see below, para **3.4.4**].

3.4.2.b It should be noted that when people claim that Holy Communion is a converting ordinance they often believe that this idea derives, in the form in which they express it, from the teaching of John Wesley, i.e that it is a proclamation of the Gospel and can elicit a response. However, Wesley's use of the phrase 'a converting ordinance' denoted his belief that someone 'seeking salvation' might find it in Communion. Baptism was none the less for him the condition for presenting oneself at Holy Communion.

3.4.2.c The many documents produced in bilateral conversations involving Orthodox, Roman Catholics and Anglicans attest that baptism should always be a precondition for the reception of Holy Communion. The practice in these and other Churches is described below [**4.1 – 4.6**].

3.4.3 Preparation

It is often objected that children should not be admitted to Holy Communion because they do not *understand* what they are doing. Adults, however, do not *understand* in any ultimate sense what happens at the Lord's Table, but such a realisation does not mean that no attempt should be made to understand. All ought to seek understanding in the measure that is possible. Preparation to receive Communion can only be a benefit. [See the Survey **2.2.1.7.**] There is some evidence in the Survey that the discussion of the possibility of children participating in Holy Communion has raised the level of adult awareness of dimensions of sacramental theology previously neglected. There is a need for regular preaching about the Sacraments as well as for opportunity to discuss their significance in fellowship groups. Children in common with everyone else can only be enriched by being taught the significance of the Sacraments of the Gospel. The chance to speak of baptism as well as Holy Communion should be seized. Learning opportunities might appropriately be created by the minister in pastoral charge, by local preachers, and by leaders of the Junior Church, who themselves may feel the need for help in this task. This cannot be considered a one-off duty which enables children to participate in Holy Communion. It ought to become a considered part of the learning programme of the whole Church, in which understanding is honed or enlarged. Nevertheless, whilst a high level of preparation is desirable for those participating in Holy Communion, *understanding* should not in itself be considered a pre-condition.

3.4.4 Parental agreement

The Survey indicates that before children are allowed to participate in Holy Communion, more than two thirds of churches insist that the parents must either have given their consent or not objected. This raises two separate but related issues. Firstly, there are problems in the case where children come to church without their parents. Often the parents have little or no contact with the church and do not know what happens there. It may be considered unreasonable to ask them to express a view as to whether their child should receive Communion. The attempt to explain why they are being asked for permission may in itself be an evangelistic opportunity, giving access, for a focused reason, to a home which might otherwise remain unvisited. However, their rights as parents must be respected, whatever the outcome of the conversation. Secondly, there are problems of cutting across parental authority, where parents, who are present at and themselves receive Holy Communion, do not want their children to receive. Their views too must be respected. They should be encouraged to allow their children to accompany them to the communion rail to be offered a blessing. Nevertheless parents should always be encouraged to take seriously the rights and opinions of the child in reaching their own conclusions.

3.4.5 Age

The table at 2.2.2.4 shows that the likelihood of a child being offered the bread and wine increases with the child's age. Guideline D [1987 Report] states that the Church has a responsibility to discriminate and test but this must not become the opportunity for adults to deprive children of 'the means of grace simply because they are children.'

3.5 Practice

3.5.1 How widespread is the practice of children being present during the service of Holy Communion?

The table at 2.2.2.1 shows that the vast majority (87%) of churches surveyed allow children to be present at some point during the service of Holy Communion.

3.5.2 For which parts of the service are they present?

The table at 2.2.2.2 shows that where children are present at some point in the normal Communion service, just under two thirds of them witness the sharing of bread and wine. A third are not present for the prayer of thanksgiving and the distribution of the elements. They do not experience the climax of the liturgy. Whether children receive a blessing or the bread and wine, it is vital to a child's spiritual development that s/he should experience the moment when, receiving the Body of Christ, the Body of Christ is built up in faith and unity. Family Communion Services are relatively infrequent. Additional opportunities should be given for children to be present at the climax of the service.

3.5.3 Use of local liturgy

The table at 2.2.2.3 shows that whilst the Sunday Service was being widely used at Family Communions, other books or the local church's own liturgy are also being used quite extensively. This variety reflects a tension within the whole Church between on the one hand ensuring consistency of theology in our liturgy and not wishing on the other to stifle the creativity of those who wish to use their own words. There could be a proliferation of liturgies that could be theologically inadequate. The Conference guidelines on the creation of local liturgies will be helpful here and the advent of the Methodist Worship Book may change the situation radically.

3.5.4 Provision of support material

The Methodist Worship Book contains a number of services of Holy Communion, at all of which it is hoped that children will at some time be present. With such variety it is not possible to produce a single illustrated order of service of the kind previously available. Other ways of providing support material for children are being developed.

3.6   The place of the blessing in Holy Communion

Although the survey conducted supports the conclusion that it is time to move forward and encourage children to participate fully in the Lord's Supper, it still remains an option that anyone, young or old, may come and seek a blessing when he or she is not able or does not wish, for whatever reason, to receive the elements. Blessing itself is a many-layered concept with rich tones which needs to be rescued from trivialization. It is a celebration of the presence of God in and with his world, which in essence includes all people. There is no single, finished definition of blessing in the Scriptures but it is best understood in terms of gift, building as it does on categories of relationship, presence and community solidarity. It is available to all, however tentative their faith in God, including, in our secular society, those whose belief is a mere residual trace. It would make no sense for someone who categorically refuses belief in God to offer himself or herself for blessing, i.e. ask God to make actual that potential which lies within them. It is, however, entirely appropriate for a person of faith to say words of blessing to others as an expression of the fact that God is with them even if the person receiving the blessing does not reciprocate God's offer of relationship. Blessing is a declaration of God's purpose for his children. It is the assertion that God is favourably disposed towards all, that nobody is excluded from God's intention. God wants everyone and everything he has made to flourish, grow and prosper. To bless someone in the name of God, for it is always God who blesses, is to declare to those addressed that they share an inheritance which is offered to all.

4   PRACTICE IN OTHER CHURCHES

Baptism and Church Membership with particular reference to Local Ecumenical Partnerships (CTE 1997) explores issues of Baptism, membership and admission to Communion among those churches which are frequent partners in LEPs. At least four different patterns of initiation are noted. All these patterns involve a process of initiation which includes different elements (God's call to faith, preparation, nurture, prayer for the gift of the Spirit, profession of faith, baptism, reception into membership of the church, admission to Communion) but in varying sequence.

4.1   The Orthodox Churches

In the Orthodox churches, baptism and chrismation [anointing with oil consecrated by a bishop] is immediately followed by admission to Communion, at whatever age a person is baptized. Infant baptism, with chrismation and first Communion, is the norm. The importance of the link between baptism, chrismation and Communion is shown by the fact that, when baptism does not take place at a time when Holy Communion is being celebrated, those who have been baptized and anointed are given the elements from the reserved sacrament. The Orthodox practice is close to that of the early Church, in which baptism, anointing [and/or laying on of hands] and admission to Communion were part of a unified rite of Christian initiation.

4.2   The Roman Catholic Church

One Bread, One Body [1998], a teaching document on the Eucharist in the life of the Church, issued by the Catholic Bishops' Conference of England and Wales, Ireland and Scotland, urges Catholics 'to refresh and renew their belief in the Eucharist, their understanding of Catholic teaching, and their reverence for this great mystery of faith.' The document describes Baptism as 'the gateway to life in the Spirit, and the door which gives access to the other sacraments. It is a point of departure, a sacred beginning to membership of the Pilgrim Church... Receiving Holy Communion is the climax of the process of initiation begun by Baptism.' [18]

'At nearly every Catholic celebration of Mass there are people in differing degrees of spiritual and visible communion with the community gathered there... who know that they are taking part in a real way even though they may not receive Communion. There are unbaptized people being prepared to be initiated into the Church, as well as baptized Christians on the way towards Reception into Full Communion with the Catholic Church. There are young children who are not yet ready to receive their first Holy Communion.' [42]

'When young children make their first Holy Communion, they too are brought into a new and deepened communion with the Catholic Church.' [54]

In the Roman Catholic Church in England and Wales it is usual for baptized children to be prepared to receive their 'First Communion' at the age of 7 or 8. Confirmation normally follows after further specific teaching and preparation in the early teens. In the Salford diocese, however, there is a practice of confirming at about the age of seven children who are only then admitted to Communion for the first time.

4.3   The Church of England

The House of Bishops of the Church of England has issued guidelines on the admission of baptized persons to Holy Communion before confirmation (GS 1212). Guideline C states, "Before admitting a person to Communion, the priest must seek evidence of Baptism. Baptism always precedes admission to Communion." This absolute requirement of Baptism carries weight in Local Ecumenical Partnerships involving Anglicans. The issue is highlighted in LEPs where eucharistic forms of worship may be held as the main Sunday morning service on two or three weeks out of four.

4.4   Baptist Churches

In Baptist churches there is little evidence of the desire for or expectation that children will be admitted to Communion prior to Believers' Baptism. Services of Holy Communion are normally held roughly once a month. Whether to offer bread and wine to those not baptized is a matter for congregational decision.

4.5   The Church of Scotland

In the Church of Scotland a growing number of local congregations are deciding to admit baptized children to Communion prior to their being received into membership. This trend is accompanied by a move towards more frequent eucharistic celebration.

4.6   The United Reformed Church

The United Reformed Church offers two routes to full membership of the church: by infant baptism and later confirmation, or by believers' baptism incorporating confirmation. Local congregations are encouraged to consider the admission of baptized children to Communion before confirmation and to determine local policy. A significant number of congregations are doing so, though local practice varies. This is a live issue within the United Reformed Church.

4.7   Recommendations of report of Churches Together in England - *Baptism and Church Membership*

The ecumenical working party recommended inter alia:

4.7.1   The child in the church

We recommend that this renewed concern about the place of the child in the church, with the Christian nurture of children and the whole catechetical process, should be tackled by the churches working together [Recommendation 39].

4.7.2   The admission of children to Communion

We invite all churches to take the situation of LEPs into account as they come to a mind on the admission of young children to Communion [Recommendation 90].

It is also recommended that clear agreements should be established on admission of children to Communion before LEP constitutions are drawn up or when they are reviewed [Recommendation 65 (a) and (b)].

The need for pastoral sensitivity and a degree of flexibility in difficult cases was recognised [Recommendation 65 (c)].

5   FUTURE METHODIST POLICY

RECOMMENDATIONS

5.1   that it be considered normal practice for baptized children, as members of the whole Body of Christ, to participate in Holy Communion by receiving bread and wine, irrespective of age.

The 1987 Guidelines encouraged Church Councils to allow children to participate fully in the Lord's Supper. Many churches have adopted this practice but others have not. As a result we have a diversity of practice across the connexion leading to pastoral anomalies which cause misunderstanding and distress. Also for good theological and pastoral reasons once a child has been admitted to Holy Communion the decision ought not to be reversed, except for matters of discipline. Where children have been fully admitted to Communion there have been widespread spiritual benefits for the whole congregation. The time has come for these benefits to be experienced across the whole connexion. The worthiness of anyone to receive the Body and Blood of Christ is based solely on the grace of God. A baptized person has by the grace of God been incorporated into the Body of Christ, his Church. It is appropriate therefore that any baptized member of the Body be fed. Conditions relating to age and level of understanding should be set aside.

5.2 that children and adults who receive Holy Communion, if not already baptized, be encouraged to be baptized

'Baptism marks entry into the One Catholic and Apostolic Church' (*The Methodist Worship Book,* page 60). The 1987 Guidelines 'expected as a theological principle that a child to be admitted to communicant participation in the Lord's Supper will have been baptized'. That principle should be maintained and should be applied, of course, to adults as well as to children. The 1987 Guidelines also stated that 'if, from time to time, it is judged appropriate for unbaptized children to be admitted to the Lord's Supper, it is expected that, after due consideration, baptism will follow'. That expectation should also remain, and again should apply both to children and to adults. It is inconceivable that a person holding out her/his hands would, at that moment, be refused bread and wine. If it is subsequently discovered that an unbaptized person, of whatever age, has presented himself/herself at Holy Communion, a pastoral conversation should follow without undue delay.

The survey reveals that only a small number of Methodist churches have followed the 1987 Guidelines in recognizing the connection between entry into the Church through baptism and receiving Holy Communion, though the figure is substantially higher in LEPs (see 2.2.2.5). The publication of this report provides an opportunity for all churches to ensure that their practice accords with the connexional policy set out in the above recommendation.

5.3 that opportunities for learning about the significance of the Sacraments be a considered and integrated part of the Church's life

The consideration of the meaning of baptism as well as the significance of the Lord's Supper would help local congregations to take seriously the relationship between the two. Adequate preparation of both children and adults to receive baptism and to participate regularly in the celebration of Holy Communion requires the use of appropriate study material.

5.4 that the consent of a child's parents be sought before that child is allowed to receive the elements

The responsibilities of parents must be maintained even when they come to a decision which the members of the local congregation regret. The possibility of causing strife in the home by the mere raising of the question has to be recognized and handled sensitively. How the consent of the parents is sought will also need careful thought locally. The opportunity of visiting the home with the possibility of serious conversation about a central Christian issue should not be neglected. Yet it is also very important to acknowledge that children, too, have a legitimate point of view. Their voice should be heard and given due weight in conversations which relate to them.

5.5   that Methodist members of Local Ecumenical Partnerships be asked to exercise *'Ecumenical Restraint'* rather than cause undue difficulties for sisters and brothers in another denominational tradition by insisting on their freedom in this matter

There are many documents emerging in many Churches nowadays seeking the admission of children to Holy Communion. Some have not yet come to a conclusion. Methodists might hope that the production and adoption of this report will lead to a wider ecumenical agreement, but for the moment accept the constraints which our relationships with other Churches impose.

5.6   that more opportunities be provided for adults and children to share together in the whole service of Holy Communion.

Holy Communion is the focal act of Christian worship, where the Body of Christ is gathered. Adults and children should be able to receive Holy Communion together whenever it is celebrated. Children need to experience the service in its wholeness.

RESOLUTION

42/1.   The Conference adopts the report and directs the Methodist Council to arrange for the production of "appropriate study material", identified as necessary in Recommendation 5:3, paying particular attention to the needs of the increasing number of those people who, in our contemporary "post Christian" society, come to "belong" before they "believe".

The Role and Recognition of Evangelists in the Methodist Church

The past ten years have been marked by the Christian denominations as a Decade of Evangelism and this has put the evangelistic task firmly on church agendas. Its importance has been further underlined by the continuing decline in church membership across most of the major denominations. The Methodist Church at the beginning of the 21st century faces a situation different from that during most of its history. Society has changed, and the predominant culture is now a secularized, post-modern and post-Christian one in which we can no longer assume that people have any basic Christian knowledge or understanding. If the need in earlier years was to call people back to faith, the need today is for forms of primary evangelism which start much further back and assume nothing. We have entered a new missionary era which makes the importance of discovering, developing and deploying those within the church who have evangelistic gifts a vital and urgent need.

1. UNDERSTANDING THE TASK

1.1 All mission is God's mission. The influential Conference report *Sharing in God's Mission (1985)* put it thus:

> 'There is only one mission to the world that matters and that is God's continuous activity of caring for and reaching out to all that he has made. By mission we mean any way in which Christians are sent to share in experiencing and expressing that love. It involves *evangelism* since God has declared his desire for all mankind to know and love him. It includes *social caring* for God's mercy reaches out especially for the poor and needy. It incorporates the political *struggle for justice* in our society because God intends men and women to live at peace together. These three do not exhaust the missionary task, neither are they alternatives in our mission, for they belong inextricably together. They are imperatives, not options'.

1.2 That holistic understanding of the church's mission has been echoed in many other Methodist reports since:

> *The Ministry of the People of God in the World (1990)* argued for forms of ministry focused more on witness and discipleship than on servicing the structures of the church.

> *Dialogue and Evangelism Among People of Other Faiths (1994)* put the mission task in its proper multi-faith context, but also recognised that 'God has called some to be evangelists, whose vocation is not only to share the story of Jesus but also to commend

him to others as Lord and Saviour . . . The church must affirm that calling'.

A Statement of Purpose (1996) (Part 1, *The Calling of the Methodist Church*) expressed the task in the following terms: 'Methodism endorses many dimensions and methods of Christian mission. In particular it affirms that mission includes:

- Telling the good news of Jesus
- Calling people to faith in Jesus Christ and to Christian discipleship
- Caring for individual people and communities
- Sharing in the task of education and social and spiritual development
- Struggling for a just world
- Being alongside the poor
- Becoming friends with people of different cultures and faiths
- Caring for the earth
- Building partnerships with other churches and other groups who share some of our mission aims'.

Those different approaches are complementary strands of a seamless whole and they require a variety of gifts and emphases. We need people whose primary focus will be on one or other of these tasks, though we all go on affirming all of them to be important. Thus the first two clearly point to the need for some within the life of the church whose particular gifting and experience is in the area of evangelism. Indeed, that is the clear implication of one of the four major assertions about the purpose of the church contained in the new vision statement for the Methodist Church, *Our Calling,* adopted at the Conference of 2000: 'The Church exists to make more followers of Jesus Christ'.

For discussion

Look again at the things listed above in the *Statement of Purpose.* How many of them apply to your local church as well as to the connexional team, and who can you identify in your congregation who is particularly gifted and active in each of these areas of work?

1.3 Perhaps surprisingly, the word 'evangelism' does not appear in the Bible at all. However, 'evangelists' are referred to three times (Acts 21:8, Ephesians 4:11 and 2 Timothy 4:5); the verb *euaggelizesthai* (to 'evangelise') occurs frequently; and the related noun *euaggelion* ('gospel') is so fundamental that it crops up all over the pages of the New Testament. It is not entirely clear how 'evangelists' were defined, but what is beyond question is that in a variety of pioneering and innovative ways the early Christian leaders (whether termed 'evangelists' or not) and the whole Christian community (by their lifestyle and everyday witness) articulated God's good news in Jesus Christ with such conviction and commitment that many others were brought to faith.

1.4 It is clear that evangelists (alongside apostles, prophets, pastors, teachers and those with a variety of other gifts) were equipped and empowered by the Holy Spirit for the church's mission and ministry, and that their gifts were used both inside and outside the church. Passages like Romans 12:4-8, 1 Corinthians 12:27-30 and Ephesians 4:11-13 make it clear that they were intended to function as part of a team, the Body of Christ, and not in isolation. Furthermore, whilst the Holy Spirit clearly gave some gifts as evangelists, the New Testament leaves us in no doubt that *all* Christians are called to bear witness to Christ and to share their faith with others. To argue for the recognition and use of evangelists in the contemporary church therefore in no way diminishes the calling of the whole church to be a witnessing community, any more than to suggest that to appoint some as deacons revokes the calling of every Christian to a servant ministry. On the contrary, evangelists focus, encourage and enable the vocation of all Christians to witness to God's grace and power in the gospel.

For discussion

Look up the three scripture passages which mention 'evangelists' (listed in 1.3 above) and share what you think their task would have involved. Do we still have such people in the church today, and if so how might they be used?

---

2. THE METHODIST CONTEXT

2.1 Methodism began as a missionary movement. John Wesley, in addition to his many other gifts as theologian, writer, educator, philanthropist, organiser and leader, was arguably one of the greatest evangelists the church has known. Many of the early Methodist preachers, both itinerant and local, were also gifted evangelists. In subsequent Methodist history that tradition was continued through people like Thomas Champness and Samuel Chadwick, the establishment and continuing ministry of Cliff College and the appointment of Home Mission evangelists such as Herbert Silverwood and Tom Butler. The old Home Mission Department appointed caravan missioners, and the Wesley Deaconess Order also played a significant role in pioneering evangelism both through caravan work and church planting. The growth of Central Halls was a further evangelistic strategy, and their superintendents (such as W E Sangster and many others) saw their role as both social and evangelistic. When 'separated Chairmen' were appointed to some Districts part of their role was seen as that of a 'District Missionary'. More recently the appointment of Rob Frost as a connexional evangelist has made a significant contribution to Methodism's evangelistic outreach. Thus the role of the evangelist has repeatedly been recognised by the church, and this report simply argues for a further development in this process.

2.2 Over the past decade the 'evangelist' has come to be seen less as an individual standing outside the local church (a model dominant in the 19th and early 20th centuries) and more as someone who helps a missionary-minded congregation to focus and fulfil its evangelistic task. There has been considerable growth in the number of people serving as evangelists or evangelism enablers at local, Circuit and District levels. The Methodist Conference in 1993 urged every Methodist District 'to consider appointing a District Evangelist/Mission Enabler/Team to encourage and assist churches in their evangelistic task', and in 1995 set aside connexional start-up funding for such appointments. Currently about a third of our Districts have people or teams in post and others are being considered. Provision is already made in Standing Order 405 'to appoint a lay person to undertake pastoral, evangelistic or administrative work' at District level; and SO570 makes parallel provision for such appointments at Circuit level.

For discussion

Do you know of people appointed under either of these Standing Orders to work in the area of evangelism in your District or Circuit? If so, what are their responsibilities? If not, could such an appointment be useful?

2.3 The Methodist Church has increasingly recognised a wide variety of gifts and callings and made provision for appropriate training and recognition:

> **Local Preachers** have always played an important part in Methodist life and worship, and the *Faith and Worship* material is only the latest in a succession of training courses to equip them for their task.

> For many years training has been provided for **Sunday School teachers** and other workers among children (notably through *Kaleidoscope)* and theirs has been recognised as a distinctive and important ministry.

> More recent years have seen the development of the *Spectrum* training course and official recognition for **youth workers**.

> The *Worship Leaders' Training Pack* is being increasingly widely used and found helpful.

All this is a welcome recognition of the fact that God gives different gifts to different people. The recognition and training of **evangelists** in the life of the church is simply a logical extension of this process whose time has surely come. It has been well said that what a church truly values can be deduced from what sort of people it trains.

2.4 In 1997 a major report was presented to the Methodist Conference entitled *The Making of Ministry* which opened the way for a much more flexible understanding of ministry, both lay and ordained, and underlined the importance of a variety of Christian callings. It asserted that 'theological education should be rooted and grounded in the mission of the church ... and supportive of many kinds of Christian vocation, lay or ordained' and that the theological resources of the church should 'provide training for those called to specific ministries'. The report has been widely welcomed within Methodism, and the concept of ministry it contains leaves room for the exercise of particular gifts (including those of the evangelist) in new and exciting ways.

2.5 In 1998 a further Conference report on *Connexional Training Strategies* proposed a totally new process of theological education and training. This provides for a basic Foundation Training course which is valuable and complete in itself but may also lead on to subsequent candidature and further training for presbyteral or diaconal ministry. These new strategies aim to make provision for people to explore their vocation and gifts in much more specific ways, enabling those gifted as evangelists to be identified, trained and used.

2.6 The evangelist's calling is an honourable one in its own right and the church needs to make room for those so called whether as lay workers, presbyters or deacons. Nor is the concept of the 'evangelist' to be limited to those working among younger people. Evangelists are needed to work with every age group. Indeed, faith development theory and the research published in *Finding Faith Today* (Bible Society 1992) underline the need for the evangelistic process to be an ongoing one incorporating teaching as well as challenge. For most people conversion is a process rather than a crisis.

2.7 Some ordained ministers and deacons with evangelistic gifts are keen to use them more fully, but further thought needs to be given to how they might be appointed to specifically evangelistic forms of ministry without being squeezed into a purely or predominately pastoral role. The 1999 report on *Flexible Patterns of Ministry* spoke of the need for the church to be 'more imaginative and creative in its mission and ministry'.

2.8 **Deacons** appointed to work as evangelists will do so as an outworking of the diaconal roles outlined in the ordinal, and in particular of their vocation to serve people at the interface between the Christian community and the wider world: 'Gather in the outcasts, welcome the stranger, seek the lost'.

2.9 As for **ministers**, they are ordained to exercise a leading and directing role in enabling the church to fulfil its purposes of worship and mission. Their work is focused in the oversight of the ministry of the Word and sacraments and of pastoral charge, and they exercise that oversight by performing some functions of mission, worship and pastoral care themselves. Being an evangelist comes primarily into the area of the ministry of the Word, and it ought to be possible for ministers to be appointed to that role as their primary function whilst still fulfilling some sacramental and pastoral responsibilities.

2.10 All of this needs to be set in its ecumenical context. The Church of England has formally established a College of Evangelists (a 'fellowship' or 'network' rather than an institution) with the first 25 evangelists commissioned by the Archbishops of Canterbury and York in October 1999. Representatives of the Baptist, Methodist and United Reformed churches as well as the Churches Together in England Group for Evangelisation have kept in close touch with the Anglican Board of Mission over these developments. There are also lessons to be learnt from our world church partners: a number of Methodist Churches overseas, particularly in Africa, have both lay and ordained 'Evangelists' – sometimes even an Order of Evangelists – and we might learn from their experience.

For discussion

What examples do you know of ministers or deacons whose gifts as evangelists or evangelism enablers are being imaginatively and effectively used by the church? In what ways could we be more creative in the use of such gifts in our own Circuit staff?

---

3. QUESTIONS TO BE EXPLORED

Mention of the word 'evangelist' unfortunately opens the flood-gates for all sorts of stereotypes, misconceptions and caricatures – some of which, indeed, have resulted from over-zealous and inappropriate approaches to evangelism by the evangelists themselves. During much of the 20th century the word was perhaps predominantly associated with mass evangelism and well-known names which resulted in local evangelists, especially those gifted in reaching people on a more one-to-one basis, being overlooked or marginalised. A further problem has been that evangelists, finding little opportunity for employment within the denominational structures, have often gone to para-church agencies or become freelance entrepreneurs. Those called and gifted in this way represent different theological persuasions (we must resist the idea that one has to be an evangelical to be an evangelist) and a wide variety of approaches: some are preachers, others are more at home in visitation, pastoral evangelism, leading groups, personal faith sharing or working alongside young or older people. Some evangelists travel widely whereas others function within a church or Circuit and are unknown beyond it.

For discussion

Share frankly how you react to the word 'evangelist' and why. How can we avoid its more negative overtones in the way we use evangelists in the Methodist Church?

The role and use of evangelists in the Methodist Church undoubtedly raises many questions, therefore, and these need to be faced. In particular, we identify the following specific issues:

a. **Calling**

The question of calling is linked with that of definition. What is an evangelist? The Anglican report *Good News People* understands the word 'evangelist' in the following terms:

"Someone, man or woman, lay or ordained:

- who goes where the church is not.
- who proclaims and lives the gospel: the way in which this 'proclamation' takes place is essentially contextual - and is by no means limited to preaching or even to verbal communication.
- who interprets the church to the world and the world to the church.
- who comes from the centre of the church and feeds from its riches and is accountable to it as well as challenging it.
- who encourages the whole church in its work of evangelism, not least by communicating the gospel to those inside as well as outside the church".

We would endorse that description, though would want to sharpen it in two particular ways. First, we need to recognise the importance of *giftedness*: being an evangelist is not simply the exercise of a personal interest or enthusiasm, but a response to the calling and equipping of the Holy Spirit. Second, we would want to add something about the importance of *fruitfulness*: an evangelist is not only one who proclaims the gospel, but who is used by God in leading people to respond to it. An evangelist whose ministry leads no-one to faith is like an angler who never catches any fish!

The need for evangelists in the church remains, and the fact that people are still being gifted in that way in the contemporary church cannot be denied. We need therefore to devise ways of testing those called as evangelists, perhaps in ways parallel to the testing of those called as

106

local preachers, worship leaders or lay workers. For them the testing takes place largely at local church or Circuit level and this would seem to be appropriate for evangelists also. Even if they go on to serve at District or connexional level their calling needs first to be tested locally. A distinction needs to be drawn between those who are formally employed within the church (whether as Lay Workers under SO405 or 570, or as Ministers or Deacons) and those who will serve in a purely voluntary capacity. Yet for both the same criteria will need to be applied. These might include:

i. Active membership of the local church and involvement in its life, worship and witness.

ii. A genuine personal experience of Jesus Christ and a disciplined spiritual life.

iii. A self-evident commitment to the work of evangelism and some understanding of the breadth of approaches and methods which might be adopted.

iv. A mature understanding of the gospel and the way in which it relates to and interacts with individuals and contemporary society.

v. The ability to relate naturally and easily to other people both within and beyond the church.

vi. Proven gifts as a communicator of the gospel and the ability to express its message in a variety of imaginative ways, especially to those unused to Christian insights and vocabulary.

vii. Evidence of some fruitfulness in terms of effectiveness and the response of others to their previous evangelistic work.

It has been increasingly recognised in recent years that every local church needs a pastor. Perhaps it is equally important for every local church to have an evangelist. If the decline of the church is to be reversed and the gospel is to be spread effectively this possibility certainly needs to be explored further. Yet it should not simply be the prerogative of the evangelist to announce his or her availability to the church. There is much to be said (and clear biblical precedent - see Acts 13:1-3) for the local church taking the initiative, identifying and calling out those within its membership who have evangelistic gifts.

For discussion

Do you agree with what is outlined above about how an evangelist's calling might be tested? Have you alternative suggestions to make? How formal should the process be made?

---

b. **Training**

Just as the Methodist Church has provided training for other forms of service so, too, adequate provision needs to be made for those called as evangelists. There is already a great deal of training on offer through colleges and courses both within and beyond Methodism. Most of it, however, is on the subject of 'mission' understood very broadly, rather than specifically on evangelism, and is of a biblical, theological and historical nature without offering the more practical training which is also required by those serving as evangelists. Other training is available from:

i.   **Cliff College**: Foundation, certificate, diploma, degree and post-graduate courses in Biblical and Evangelistic Ministry.

ii. **The Open Learning Centre** at Cliff College: a diploma course in evangelism developed in collaboration with St John's College, Nottingham.

iii. **Other Bible colleges**: courses in evangelism at St John's College, Nottingham, Spurgeons College, London Bible College and other institutions.

iv. **Other organisations and agencies**: published material suitable for basic training in evangelism includes resources from the Church Pastoral Aid Society, Scripture Union, the Bible Society, Grove Books and others.

Since evangelists are likely to be working in different ways and at many different levels within the Methodist Church it is probably unnecessary to insist on any one form of training, although there would be great value in producing a basic training course parallel to *Kaleidoscope, Spectrum* and the *Worship Leaders' Training Pack*. For now, some way needs to be devised of assessing individual needs and pointing people in the direction of existing training which is appropriate to them and the work they are to do. Such training should include the theology and practice of evangelism, apologetics, cultural awareness (including the inter-faith perspective) and communication skills.

Training needs to be both initial and continuing. The twice-yearly meetings of the Forum for Methodist Evangelists can play an important part here by providing fellowship and support networks, information and training; but training should also be available within the Districts as is currently the case for Lay Workers.

For discussion

Do you think the various sorts of training outlined above are adequate? Have any members of your congregation/ Circuit/District been trained in any of these ways? Are there others whom you might encourage to seek such training, and what would be most appropriate for them?

---

c. **Recognition**

A specific 'Order' of evangelists is unnecessary, but some means is needed of enabling evangelists to be affirmed and formally recognised by the church. This is perhaps easier for those who are to be officially employed whether at Circuit, District or connexional level; but the need applies to all who are called to work as evangelists in whatever capacity. It would be appropriate for an evangelist to be formally recognised at the level of church life in which he/she was to work, but there would need to be some standard form of recognition and authorization which applied to all. This might be helped by devising and authorizing a commissioning service parallel to those now available in the *Methodist Worship Book* for lay workers, pastoral visitors and workers with children and young people, and perhaps also a new Service of Commissioning for special periods of evangelistic outreach by the church. This would have the effect of raising awareness of the appointment and work of evangelists and affording them recognition within both the structural and liturgical life of the church.

For discussion

Are the suggestions outlined above appropriate and adequate? In what other ways do you think the Methodist Church might give formal recognition to those called and trained as evangelists or evangelism enablers?

---

d. **Accountability**

With official recognition comes the need for ensuring some form of accountability for evangelists. Since this report envisages evangelists as working within the structures of the church at local, District or connexional level rather than independently, this makes the matter of oversight rather more straightforward. It is important from the evangelist's point of view to have adequate structures for support, guidance and accountability; and it is important from the church's point of view to have a clear set of procedures for oversight and, if necessary, discipline. Thus for an evangelist working in a local church context, the Church Council would be the appropriate oversight body; in a Circuit it would the Circuit Meeting; District evangelists or evangelism enablers would be accountable to the District Policy Committee; and for evangelists working at connexional level (currently only Rob Frost and the staff evangelists at Cliff College) accountability would be through the Methodist Council or the Cliff College Committee.

Evangelists who are ordained ministers or deacons would have the normal forms of accountability through their District Synod and any other oversight and support structure which was devised in connection with their work. Those employed by the church as lay evangelists should have contracts in line with the terms and conditions laid down for Lay Workers in the Methodist Church together with support and oversight groups appropriate to their particular context. The Forum for Methodist Evangelists might well take on a more significant role in terms of establishing common standards of practice and offering a network for mutual accountability.

e. **Role**

In arguing for the recognition of evangelists in the Methodist Church it is important to reiterate and underline two points made earlier:

> The task of evangelism is only part of the overall mission of the church (see 1.1) and those engaged in it must see their role in that wider context.

> Evangelism is the task of the whole church (see 1.4). Every local church is called to be a missionary congregation and every Christian is called upon to be a witness to Jesus Christ. Evangelism must not simply be left to the evangelists.

The evangelist, however, is one who is especially gifted in sharing the Christian gospel with others so as to win a response of faith, and has been released and authorised to exercise those gifts. In so doing he or she might act both as an evangelist and as an evangelism enabler - encouraging, training and resourcing others to engage in the church's evangelistic task. This raises the question of whether the 'Evangelism Enabler' comes within the purview of this report, and whether it is essential for such an Enabler also to be an Evangelist. We believe both roles to be important and complementary, and would want both to be embraced in the provisions outlined in the preceding pages. A further question is whether it would be expected that an evangelist was a Local Preacher, but we do not envisage that being a requirement. There are many other forms of evangelism besides preaching.

The precise work of an evangelist (or evangelism enabler) will vary with the nature of the appointment, but some or all of the following may well be part of that role.

i. Helping local churches to develop holistic outreach strategies
ii. Advising on formulating mission statements
iii. Leading faith-sharing training courses
iv. Offering guidance on youth and children's outreach
v. Running a Holiday Bible Club
vi. Organising circuit evangelistic events
vii. Evangelistic preaching and speaking
viii. Suggesting books and training materials on evangelism
ix. Sharing stories about effective evangelism elsewhere
x. Providing information about national evangelism initiatives
xi. Developing, training and leading mission teams
xii. Outreach visitation
xiii. Baptismal preparation

    xiv. Running an Alpha or Emmaus course
    xv. Developing contemporary alternative worship services
    xvi. Planting a new congregation

This is not to provide an exhaustive list, but to indicate some of the different ways in which evangelists might be used. There is growing evidence that many churches want to take evangelism seriously but do not know how to set about it. The appointment of more evangelists and evangelism enablers would be a significant step in providing the help they need and equipping the church to face the urgent missionary challenge of the 21st century.

For discussion

How do you react to this report as a whole? Do you agree with its basic thrust? Have you specific comments (either positive or negative) to make on its contents, or suggestions to offer about its implementation? How do you think it might apply to the missionary challenge you face, and what difference might it make to the ways in which you tackle it in your situation?

RESOLUTIONS

The following resolutions were agreed by the Methodist Conference of 2000:

The Conference

1.   recognises the urgent missionary challenge facing the church at the start of the twenty-first century, underlines the need identified in *Our Calling to Fulfil* to make more followers of Jesus Christ, and affirms the importance of evangelism for the Church and its ministry at every level;

2.   directs the Evangelism Enabling Group to publish and circulate to the Districts and Circuits a popular version of this report* for discussion within the context of *Our Calling to Fulfil* and response by 31 December 2001, so that a final report with firm recommendations can be brought to the Conference of 2002;

3.   acknowledges the need for identifying, training and appointing those with evangelistic gifts in presbyteral, diaconal and lay ministry, and directs the Formation in Ministry Office to explore more effective ways of meeting that need, and to report to the Conference of 2002;

4.   directs the Evangelism Enabling Group in consultation with other appropriate groups and officers to develop a basic training course for evangelists and evangelism enablers and to report to the Conference of 2002;

5.   invites the Faith and Order Committee to consider what new services might need to be devised in the light of this report, and to prepare them for consideration by the Conference of 2002.

*The above report is the 'popular version' referred to. The version printed in the Conference agenda has been slightly shortened and questions for discussion have been added.

YOU ARE INVITED TO

send your comments on this report and your suggestions for its amendment and improvement to

The Rev Graham Horsley,
Evangelism Office,
Methodist Church House,
25 Marylebone Road,
London NW1 5JR

by the end of December 2001.

Scotland District Resolution

One Body with Many Parts: Report of the study group regarding the response of Methodism to devolution in the United Kingdom and associated territories.

1. **Summary.** The purpose of this study group was to consider the consequences of political devolution for Methodism's ability to respond to initiatives taken by regional/national assemblies/parliaments within the area under the authority of the British Methodist Conference. As with the home rule legislation relating to the integrity of the state, we have sought to preserve the unity of purpose and organisation of British Methodism while recognising the necessity and desirability of local responses to matters determined by sub-United Kingdom governmental institutions. The group recognised that given the diversity of powers exercised by the various regional governmental institutions, and the differing local relationships between Methodism and secular and religious bodies, it would be impossible to recommend a uniform structure, though it feels able to recommend a framework within which coherent and sensible arrangements can be established.

2. **Background Information.** Our report is in response to a District Resolution brought to the Conference in 1998 from the Scotland District, and the Conference Resolution arising from it:

    > "We value our place within the Methodist Connexion but are wary of the tensions that may ensue as political union changes. We ask the Conference to direct the Methodist Council to set up a working party, including representatives of the Scotland and Shetland Synods and Y Gymanfa, to look at the ways in which, as a connexional church, we can best respond to a Parliament of Edinburgh, an Assembly in Cardiff and possible developments in the regions of England, while continuing effectively to address public issues which remain the preserve of the Westminster Parliament and of public bodies whose remit covers Britain as a whole.

    > RESOLUTION 8/1: The Conference directs the Methodist Council to set up a Working Party as proposed by the Methodist Synod in Scotland with the constitution and remit outlined in this report, and report to the Conference of 2000."

3. The Study Group were Dr Michael Dyer (Convenor), The Revds Pamela Cram, Ian White and Stephen Caddy.

4. **Main Report**

4.1 **The Context.** Devolution or home rule is not unique to the territories under the ultimate control of the United Kingdom Crown. The Isle of Man and the Channel Islands have long exercised widespread control over their own affairs, and Scotland has enjoyed administrative devolution since 1707. Inevitably, Methodism has developed local understandings and procedures to address issues in these territories. To that extent the question being addressed is not novel.

4.2 Novelty has arisen through the creation of the Scottish Parliament and Welsh Assembly, and the possibility that regional assemblies might be introduced progressively to England. It is therefore necessary to consider how Methodism is to respond to initiatives taken by these new bodies if ad hocery, an unsatisfactory feature of current practices, is to be avoided. We were also anxious to explore ways in which Methodists living in the devolved territories might be given the opportunity to participate in the determination of Methodism's attitudes to locally determined public policy, while at the same time enabling Conference to ensure that core Methodist values remain uncompromised by political fragmentation.

4.3 Towards a Response. It was agreed that Methodism would need to respond to the new political structures, and that decision-making in the general area of domestic 'social responsibility' be regionally rather than centrally determined. The questions then arose as to what should be devolved? To whom should such matters be devolved? How should Methodism's attitudes be communicated? And what should be the role of Conference and its officers in ensuring the protection of basic positions?

4.4 What should be devolved? The management of territory in the United Kingdom has long been characterised by 'asymmetric devolution' in which the various parts have differing degrees of autonomy. Traditional rights exercised by the Isle of Man and the various Channel Islands are clearly different from those enjoyed by Scotland, whilst Welsh sensibilities, apart from church disestablishment, were essentially unrecognised before the 1960s and the creation of the Welsh Office. Recent legislation has continued the practice, with the Scottish Parliament enjoying rights over primary legislation on devolved subjects, and the Welsh Assembly restricted to secondary legislation. Regional governments in England, were they to be introduced, are likely to enjoy uniform powers, but different from those exercised by the Celtic nations. Such a 'horses for courses' approach perforce limits the development of a detailed model constitution by Conference. We are of the view, therefore, that as a general principle local Methodists should determine attitudes towards those matters which are within the remit of their local parliament/assembly.

4.5 To whom should such matters be devolved? It was a matter of some concern in our discussions that views may be expressed in the name of Methodism without any formal authority or accountability. It is therefore necessary for a formal focus to legitimate and set parameters to such exercises of individual autonomy. It is also desirable that Methodists as part of their Christian citizenship should be encouraged to concern themselves with societal issues, and devolution offers a perspective for the development of a more focused approach to social responsibility. Individual churches and circuits should not be prevented from expressing their views, as it is in keeping with the ecclesiastical principle of subsidiarity that decisions should be taken at the lowest possible level, but considerations of good order, practicality and effectiveness indicate the necessity of a more regional approach. Consequently, we consider that the synod(s) within the various governmental jurisdictions are the most appropriate bodies to which Conference should devolve power. Such a solution, however, should not deny co-operation between synods where appropriate, but it would be undesirable and self-defeating for synods to be forced into such an arrangement against their will. (We are particularly conscious of the claims of the Welsh-speaking Synod in Wales, and the Shetland District in Scotland.)

4.6 How should policy be communicated? It was clear that procedures for communicating Methodism's opinions currently vary considerably from one place to another, depending on the local political and/or ecclesiastical culture. Size is another factor: small places tend to be more informal than larger ones. We envisage that different strategies will continue, though it would be desirable for synods to make explicit what their processes are. Where there is more than one synod within a region/nation, co-operation for the communication of policy might be particularly appropriate. Ecumenical considerations also argue for a single contact, whether a designated individual or institution.

4.7 What is the role of Conference and its officers? In producing our report we were very conscious of a general desire that British Methodism should not lose its unity. However extensive was any autonomy devolved to the Districts, it might be that Conference would regard certain values as non-negotiable. Racial and gender discrimination, for example, could not be compromised. Our report does not, therefore, seek to deny Conference the ultimate right to revoke any devolved powers or to impose its will on specific matters.

4.8 We did not, however, regard central-local relations as inherently conflictual between Methodists from different parts of the United Kingdom, nor was peripheral mistrust seen as the spirit behind our group's formation, because unlike the population as a whole we share the same essential values. Rather, we see our proposals as a sensible way of lightening the load of the centre, enabling it to concentrate on core business because it can trust the parts to advance the common cause.

4.9 We particularly welcome the decision to appoint a Connexional Secretary for Parliamentary and Political Affairs, because that person can play an important role in co-ordinating the devolution programme, and act as a clearing-house for the dissemination of information.

5. Ecumenical Implications

5.1 We do not see our proposals as fundamentally changing existing relations between the churches or other faiths. They do, however, require the synods to think more systematically about existing relationships, respecting the lobbying of the various assemblies and parliaments.

6. Financial Implications

6.1 Our proposals are financially neutral. The amount of resources to be devoted to lobbying will clearly have an impact on how extensive and effective our activities are, but the size of the cloth is not our concern.

7. Recommendations

(a) That the synods within each area covered by a sub-United Kingdom Parliament/Assembly be responsible for determining Methodist attitudes towards matters within the constitutional remit of that authority, on the understanding that they work in harmony with the existing statements and resolutions of the Conference. We should learn particularly from the new ways of working in Wales brought about by Y Gymanfa under Standing Orders 412 and 491. It is not intended, however, that these Recommendations should apply to areas covered by the London Assembly or any existing or proposed English regional assembly.

(b) That the agendas of such synods routinely include a parliamentary report.

(c) That the District Secretary for Social Responsibility, or an equivalent officer, be the person responsible for devolved affairs.

(d) That wherever possible, the synods work ecumenically in their engagement with the relevant parliament/assembly.

(e) That by December 2001 the synods in any area covered by a parliament/assembly produce protocols indicating:
   i) procedures for monitoring proposals coming before their assembly/parliament
   ii) the means of determining attitudes towards policies coming before the parliament, including on-going inter-synod reactions and any consultations required by Methodist law and practice
   iii) any arrangements for inter-district co-operation.

(f) That the Conference ratifies or not the above protocols.

(g) That the Secretary for Parliamentary and Political Affairs be the appropriate person for co-ordinating devolution affairs, and receives copies of the synodical parliamentary reports.

(h) That notwithstanding the above, the Conference retains the right to over-rule decisions by the synods regarding devolved matters, and its sovereignty remains unimpaired.

RESOLUTION

57/1. The Conference adopts the report.